The Essential Vegan Travel Guide

2016 Edition

Caitlin Galer-Unti

Table of Contents

Introduction

Vegan travel? Yes you can!

• •

Picture it. You got off a 12-hour flight two hours ago and you're clutching onto the white slip of paper like it's going to save your life. You are bedraggled, and you smell like you haven't showered all day (you haven't). You haven't slept in 27 hours (thank you, screaming baby on the plane). Worse, the plane forgot your meal and you are starving. All you've had to eat in the last 15 hours is a measly bag of airplane peanuts, and a Clif bar you managed to dig up from the depths of your bag while strapped firmly into seat 28F, in between that smelly guy and the woman who kept elbowing you in the ribs every time she adjusted her seat.

You get off the train in a completely new city, and you can't even read the street signs. You clutch onto the white paper even harder, as you go up to someone in the street and try to ask them directions. When you don't understand them, you point desperately at the address on the map, then gesture wildly. International sign language for: I'm lost. Eventually, your meaning seems to get through and they point down the street, then quickly flip their hand to the right.

Thanking them over your shoulder, you stumble forward and down the side street they indicated, where you are greeted with the most beautiful sign in the world. You've never been happier in your life to see a pile of gleaming, fresh fruits and vegetables in the window of a restaurant. You practically sprint down the street toward it… But something feels wrong, a nagging feeling in the pit of your stomach. Yep, it's definitely pitch black in that restaurant, and yes, they've pulled a grate down in front of the door.

What are you going to do? You've got the following options:

1. Wander back to that restaurant you saw up the street, the one with the aggressive waiter who practically forced a menu in your hands. Sit and wait. Try and communicate with international sign language that you want a plant-based meal. How would you even begin to do that? Wait and wait and wait for them to figure out what you meant, and serve you food. Eat whatever they bring you and hope for the best, pausing occasionally to pick off bits of bacon.

2. Meander up and down the nearby streets and see if you can find a grocery store that's open. Look up and down the aisles trying desperately to find a label in English. End up buying a bunch of bananas and a tin of black beans. Eat, feeling depressed and deprived, and go to bed sort of full, but ultimately unsatisfied.

Luckily, the above scenario is a thing of the past. You are not going to starve to death, or insult local cultures, or have to survive eating beans out of cans – no matter what anyone on the internet says. You can travel and eat delicious, healthy meat-free food, in any country, and I'm going to show you how page by page in this book.*

*Except perhaps Mongolia, which has one of the most meat-heavy diets in existence. Although who knows, because as of August 2015, Happycow. net has 23 listings for vegetarian, vegan and veg-friendly restaurants and stores in Mongolia.

Who's This Book For?

This book is for anyone who's ever been frustrated or worried about finding decent food on the road. Whether you're vegan, vegetarian or a healthy eater, don't worry, you can find food on the road, and this book will show you how. We'll be focusing on finding vegan food, but you can easily adapt the advice to other dietary needs (e.g. vegetarian, gluten-free, etc.).

Their Objections – Your Solutions

"But you'll insult your hosts/host country by refusing to try their national dishes."

"But you'll never experience the real <insert country>. Everyone knows you can't really get to know a place unless you get to know their cuisine."

"What if you can't find any food? What if there aren't any vegetarian restaurants? What if you can't find any veggie options in other restaurants? What if you STARVE?"

All of these are real, actual sentences that you've probably heard when you've told people about your upcoming trip/plans to travel. I know I've heard them plenty of times. I've heard people twist these into reasons to start eating meat again on their travels – before even trying. Maybe you've never considered it. Perhaps you've even had a bad food-related travel experience previously, and you found yourself wandering around a foreign city, admiring the street artwork, but absolutely fricking starving, unable to find anywhere offering decent food that fits with your diet and lifestyle. But let's unpack each of these arguments just a little bit.

"But you'll insult your hosts/host country by refusing to try their national dishes." This is an irrelevant argument, because usually the people who utter this nonsense are exactly the sort of people you KNOW would never go to Mexico and try grasshopper tacos, or one of the various insect-inspired foods in Thailand. Also, I'm sure there are lots of local traditions that even non-vegans might refuse to participate in – like bullfighting, child marriage or stoning gay people. Now, people may not understand why you don't eat animal products, especially in a culture without a history of vegetarianism, but the vast majority of people understand that different cultures have different traditions, and quite often you will find they are actually very interested in getting to know more about your culture and beliefs, including your diet. Even if you do run the risk of offending someone, somewhere, what is better – potentially risking offending a stranger, or going against your values and consuming a food that is the product of suffering and the cause of environmental destruction? If you regularly turn down these foods at home when friends and family offer them, why stop just because you're somewhere else?

"But you'll never experience the real <insert country>. Everyone knows you can't really get to know a place unless you get to know their cuisine." A vast majority of people won't eat any and all local foods anyway. If someone asks you this, you can just retort, "Would you eat mealworms? Or cow testicles? Or an egg that's rotten and been buried for years?" (All local delicacies in some parts of the world!) Would they tell someone who's got celiac disease to avoid Italy because pasta is traditionally made with wheat flour (even though you can get a lot of gluten-free products in Italy these days)? I hope not! Besides, food is an important part of most cultures, sure, but is it the be all and end all? No! There's a lot more to experience of other cultures than just pastas, tapas or dim sum. There's also history, artwork, architecture and museums, to name but a few aspects.

"What if you can't find any food? What if there aren't any vegetarian restaurants? What if you can't find any veggie options in other restaurants? What if you STARVE?"

With a little bit of advance planning, this won't be an issue. And don't worry – over the course of this book, I'm going to show you exactly how to do this, from what websites and tools to use, to what to search for. So that no matter where you go, you will always be able to arrive with a list in hand of restaurants to try that will serve you according to your diet. Your own personal mini guidebook, if you will. And if you can't find any restaurants using the various tools outlined here, we'll go through other options. Like where to stay and what to eat in emergency situations. And even how to cook those beans in a coffeemaker in your hotel room.

Vegans Do It Better

Travel, that is. I'm going to put this out there: I enjoy travel even more as a vegan. Sure, maybe my restaurant choices are more limited, but that means I have to be choosier with where I eat. It means I can't just settle down at the first (likely overpriced, tourist-trap) restaurant I find. And I eat so much better for it.

Did I mention you're much less likely to have food poisoning as a vegan? (Just be careful about uncooked vegetables in countries where you're told to avoid the tap water.)

Oh, and you know what else? Vegan food tends to be lighter and healthier fare so you will feel less of that "oh god, I've overeaten and had so much fat and salt and feel so gross" vacation feeling.

Travel's all about discovery, feeling like you've found some corner of the world. There's no better feeling than feeling like you just discovered a vegan gem, or a fantastic vegan option hidden in a place you'd never have expected.

Travel's also all about connection. And you know what is a great way to feel connected to some stranger in a faraway place? Knowing you share a set of beliefs and a lifestyle. This far exceeds any benefit of "trying local cuisine". You'll get to try veganized versions of local cuisine and, if you're lucky, make new friends while you're at it. Vegans I've only just met have invited me to their homes, to stay with them, and to their birthday parties.

Finally, vegan restaurants are often in far-flung areas (the counterculture part of town, or a local uni campus) so you will get way out of the generic tourist areas, and see a part of the city other tourists are unlikely to see.

Okay, But How Do I Do It?

By now you realize that not only is it possible to travel and find great healthy, plant-based food, but that it's actually a great experience and will allow you to explore aspects of a local culture you wouldn't see otherwise. But how do you actually go about it? Well, using this little thing called the internet. Twenty-five years ago, you would have had to go to the library, or one of those places that sold books before we all downloaded them on the internet/Kindles. (Remember those things? They're called bookstores.) Then you would have to hope to find some sort of vegetarian guidebook on the place you were visiting. Or in the early days of the internet, like two of my friends, maybe you'd have found someone on ICQ or another chatroom who was also vegan and who owned such a guidebook on being vegetarian or vegan in Paris, and who could individually fax every single page of said book. Which sounds like a pain. Although on the other hand, that seems to create a lifelong, lasting friendship, at least in the case of my friends, who don't even live in the same country but have visited each other every year since their ICQ exchange.

These days, we have this place brimming with information about every corner of the world, which you can use to your advantage, so long as you know how. Relax, sit back, and grab a soy latte or your favorite green tea, because in the coming pages I'll be showing the tips and tricks I've acquired finding vegan food in the places I've traveled (28 countries and counting!).

We'll start off with some research methods (including some tricks I learned in my other career, researching incredibly niche blogs all over the world, from laundry blogs in Singapore to Nigerian Olympic sports blogs). Then we'll look how to make connections with locals and make new friends, then work on how to put together the list of restaurants we've pulled together. We'll look at how to choose where to stay, as well as an overview of the pros and cons of various types of accommodation. We'll then prepare you for the trip, including how to eat on the plane and what to pack. We'll look at what to do when you get there, including tips for traveling with non-vegans and how to order at non-vegetarian restaurants, and what to do if you get stuck. Last, I give you a few recipes that you can make in a holiday rental kitchen or even a hotel room. Consider this your food travel manual, a "how to" on surviving and thriving, wherever you end up in world, whether it's a quick weekend escape to a nearby city, a week-long vacation in Istanbul, or even moving abroad.

Before we start planning your trip, we need to make a list of search terms we'll use throughout our research in Sections 1 and 2. I want you to make a list (on a piece of paper, like an old-fashioned person/hipster, or in Evernote, if you wanna be high-tech about it) of all the words you can think of related to your diet that might be helpful in searching for restaurants. Hang on to this, because you'll need it in the coming sections of this chapter. Let me help you get started on your brainstorming:

Vegan

Vegetarian

Veg

Veggie

Plant-based

Healthy

Meat-free

Dairy-free

Etc.

Got your list? Okay, great! We're ready to go.

* * *

Section 1:

How the Hell Do I Find Somewhere to Eat?

Now that we've got our list of search terms, we're ready to start planning your trip. We're going to work under the assumption that you've already got a destination picked out (if not, check out the Top 10 Vegan Destinations of 2016 at the end of this book for inspiration). Rather than start out by choosing where to stay, we're going to focus on looking up vegetarian and vegan restaurants. Once you're familiar with where the restaurants are, then we'll move on to choosing a place to stay in Section 4.

We'll start with Google, then move on to vegetarian restaurant directories like HappyCow and others, local sites and blogs. Finally, we'll discuss how to make your own map and save it for offline use (in case you need to turn off your data while abroad).

Google Research

Why Google? Simply because it's the most widely used search engine. However, you can use the search engine of your choice. Just bear in mind that it might have slightly different methods to the Google ones we discuss in this section.

I'd suggest starting with a standard Google search, but you can also limit the timeframe if you just want recent results.

If you find a great site, you can use Google's "related" function, which finds sites similar to the URL you enter. You just enter "related:" followed by the URL. So for example, if you found veganlondon.co.uk and decided you liked it and wanted to find similar sites, you would type "related:veganlondon.co.uk" and it comes up with HappyCow London listings, an article in the Huffington Post on the top vegetarian restaurants in London, a Time Out feature on veggie eateries, etc. This is a very handy tool after you find a useful site or two!

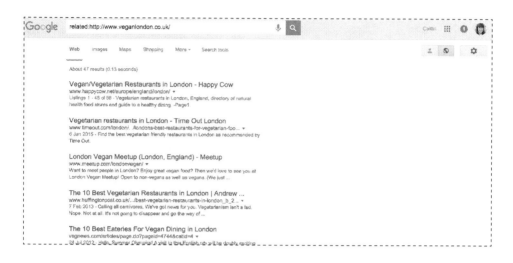

Have a play with Google, until you get a list of websites. If you're going to a city with a large vegan or vegetarian population, you'll likely find a local vegetarian organization or even a website dedicated to vegan/vegetarian living in that city. This ultra-specific resource will be your new best friend, especially if it's carefully kept up to date! You'll likely also come across articles in local publications covering the best vegetarian/vegan restaurants.

Have a look at these rankings and see if there are any special restaurants you want to treat yourself to. You can also go onto Google maps, and search "vegan" or "vegetarian" – in big cities you will usually end up with a handy map of vegetarian restaurants, like this:

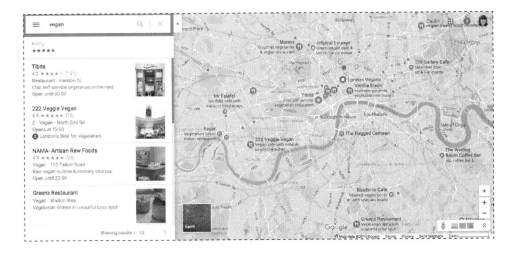

If you're going to a smaller city, or a city without a large vegetarian or vegan population, you might not come across a dedicated vegetarian or vegan organization. But if it's an area frequented by visitors, you'll likely find some blog posts or articles about visiting the area as a vegan or vegetarian. You might have to dig a bit more than you would for, say, NYC, but you can come across some good resources for vegan Santorini. You'll just need to try out more search terms, and maybe go a few pages further into Google.

If you're not having much luck with your Google search, don't give up yet. There might not be many resources out there in English! But before you finish up with Google, you should try the local version of Google. First, you'll need to find out what the Google address is for that country. For example, Google Spain is google.es, Google Brazil is google.com.br and Google Mexico is google.com.mx. It's usually some variation of either "google.com" or "google." followed by the country's two-letter ISO code. You can try guessing, or try Googling "Google Spain" or "Google Brazil". (Yes, I realize Googling Google is some sort of crazy meta-search.)

Once you're there on the local Google page, search in the local language (e.g. vegano in Spanish, végétalien in French). For example, type "Vegano Roma" into google.it. You can then further filter results into English results, Italian results, etc. Once on the individual webpage, you can auto-translate non-English sites into English (or the language of your choice) – if using Chrome, just right click and select "Translate to English."

If you're not getting many results from Google, don't worry. We're now going to delve into specific websites to use as tools. First up: HappyCow, everyone's favorite vegetarian restaurant directory!

Everyone's Favorite Site, HappyCow

Anytime you hear about vegetarian or vegan travel, you hear about HappyCow [http://happycow.com]. And with good reason. HappyCow is the most comprehensive directory of vegan, vegetarian, and vegetarian/vegan-friendly restaurants and stores around the world. HappyCow's always the place I start. You can narrow down by continent, then country, then city and find the city you're going to, or you can even take advantage of its incredibly handy maps feature to look at all the restaurants in the city on a map.

This feature is very useful if you're trying to decide where to stay and want to find a hotel near veggie restaurants (especially ones with good brunch options!). For some reason, vegan breakfasts and brunches can often be the hardest meal of the day to come by (with so many vegetarian restaurants only opening at lunchtime). So if you can assure yourself of having a breakfast (most important meal of the day, after all), then you've set yourself off to a good start.

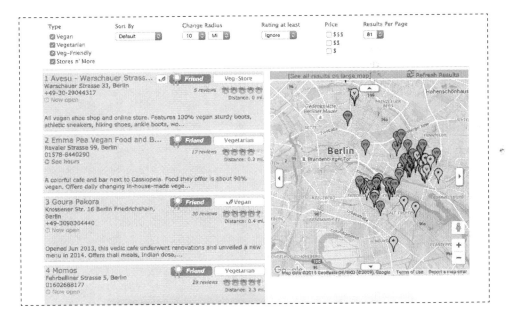

Another useful (and slightly less obvious) feature is that if you've already booked somewhere to stay, you can enter the exact address of where you're staying (or the train station you arrive at, or any other address) and then see a map, along with the closest vegetarian restaurants.

This is useful in terms of seeing options around your hotel, but also for planning your days once you're there. If, for example, you're going to the modern art museum and know you'll want to eat lunch after, you can search the location and see surrounding restaurants with veggie/vegan options.

9 Vebu
Genthiner Stra e 48, Berlin
030-20050799
☆☆☆☆☆
Distance: 0.4 mi.
Organization
Large on promoting the vegetarian and vegan lifestyle. Previously located at Glatzer Str.5, Friedrichshain.

10 Bejte Ethiopia
Zietenstrasse 8, Berlin
030-2625933
🕒 See hours
4 reviews ☆☆☆☆☆
Distance: 0.5 mi.
Veg-Friendly
Serves meat, veg options available. Religious calendar means that approximately half the year is without meat, so it's u...

11 strEats Vegan Food Truck
Wittenbergplatz, Berlin
n/a
🕒 See hours
4 reviews ☆☆☆☆☆
Distance: 0.8 mi.
Vegan
Food truck parked sometimes at this location once a week, and also at others - check webpage for updates. Serves vegan s...

12 Dolores Burritos
Bayreuther Strasse 36 Charlottenburg, Berlin
0049-30-54821590
🕒 Now open
8 reviews ☆☆☆☆☆
Distance: 0.6 mi.
Veg-Friendly
Serves meat, veg options available. California-style burritos, quesadilla, and tacos plus house-made lemonade. Has soy m...

13 Cafe Noura
Wormser Stra e 5, Berlin
+40-3023639100
🕒 Now open
1 review ☆☆☆☆☆
Distance: 0.6 mi.
Veg-Friendly
Serves meat, veg options available. Food, salad, coffee, cake, fruit, smoothies and juices; has fresh wheatgrass juice. ...

Bear in mind that HappyCow is a crowdsourced website, and its data is only as good as what its users put in. So things might be out of date sometimes, particularly in less-visited cities. It's best to Google individual restaurants before you go (good to do anyway, in case they've temporarily closed while away on their summer vacation!). Better still, phone them to check location and opening times. Remember that occasionally the information that comes up on Google that looks like this can also be out of date, if no one has informed Google of a change of address or opening times:

That's why it's best to phone the restaurant or find the restaurant's own website or Facebook page.

So, HappyCow's great, and if you've never used it, where have you been hiding? Under a lump of pink salt? But HappyCow's not the be-all and end-all – there are some other great sites out there which you should check out, as well as some iPhone/Android apps! These will make your life so much easier.

Other Directories

Apart from HappyCow, I've also had good results with VegGuide [https://www.vegguide.org]. While this may not be the best resource for planning a trip to Europe or Asia, it's great for researching restaurants in the US, and I've found that in many cities, it has even more listings than HappyCow – with one caveat: it seems to be better at listing non-vegetarian restaurants which have vegetarian and vegan options. So, this might not be the best research tool if you're looking for a romantic all-vegan restaurant in Paris for a lover's getaway, but it's great if you're traveling to Akron, Ohio (18 listings on Veg Guide vs. HappyCow's 12) with your meat-eating grandma who's not that adventurous and doesn't really fancy trying a veggie restaurant.

There is also a plethora of apps you can download on your phone, with new ones seemingly springing up all the time. The best options are HappyCow (iOS/Android $2.99-$3.99, international), Vegman (iOS, free, best for US), or Vegan Xpress (iOS, $1.99, listing of vegan options at chain restaurants across the US). These are fantastic if you have a smartphone, especially if you use the GPS for driving or walking, because most have map options where you can search for the nearest restaurants. When abroad, save cash by turning off your data and accessing the map features on the app over Wi-Fi. (In most places these days you only have to walk a few minutes to find the nearest café with free Wi-Fi!)

Local Sites

We touched on this briefly when we spoke about Google earlier – when you first Googled, you may have come across some local vegetarian or vegan sites. For example, a "vegan Mallorca" search yields this fantastic vegan Mallorca site, Mallorca Vegan [http://www.mallorcavegan.com/], which covers all the bases in Mallorca, from vegan hotels to restaurants to activities and more.

When you come across a local site, see when it was last updated – active ones are usually more up to date than HappyCow even is because they're maintained by a local who hears about all the new restaurant openings. If you're not able to find one, try searching for a vegan society/vegetarian charity for the country, and then see if they have local chapters. You may be able to find a local chapter's site – or contact – this way. For example, the North American Vegetarian Society (NAVS) maintains a list of local vegetarian chapters across North American cities. Even if they don't have restaurant listings, you can get in touch with the local chapter's contact.

If you ask nicely, they're usually willing to help out a fellow veggie, and send you some suggestions of places to eat. Who knows, you might even make a new friend who wants to go for a coffee or show you around! Like I said, sharing the lifestyle with someone is usually a great starting point and connection, and one of the best parts of travel as a vegetarian or vegan is meeting with others!

Blogs

Alright, kids, it's story time! Sit down on the rug and listen up:

Once upon a time – *well, in South Korea around the year 2009, The Traveler (that's me!) was on her first trip to Asia. She'd been to Hong Kong, China, Taiwan, and now Korea, and while she'd loved all the yummy vegan food she'd eaten so far, she was getting desperate… for a muffin. Or a cookie. Or some sort of baked good. Any would do, really. It's just she hadn't had a sweet (or a savory, to think of it) piece of floury goodness in her mouth in months. When some travelers get homesick, they go to McDonald's. Or Pizza Hut. Or an American bar. The Traveler really just needed to sit in a nice coffee shop, drinking a soy latte and eating a slice of vegan cake, as that was her true home. While searching Google, she stumbled across a blog called Alien's Day Out [http:// aliensdayout.com/], which had the answers to all her problems.*

This magnificent blog spoke of a coffee shop that not only offered soy lattes, but pumpkin and squash lattes, along with vegan cakes baked by The Blogger herself! The Traveler immediately got on the nearest train and went there without hesitating a moment. She NEEDED that coffee. When she went to order the soy pumpkin latte and the vegan cake that The Blogger had recommended in her blog post, something strange happened. A girl sitting at a nearby table stared at her, intrigued, and eventually called out, "You don't happen to be a reader of my blog, do you?"

They started talking, and made plans to meet up and go to a market, where The Blogger helped her order delicious vegan delights which she never would have been able to try on her own, not speaking a word of Korean, and then they went to a lantern festival, which The Traveler never would have found on her own. The Blogger also informed The Traveler that there was a new vegan restaurant near her hostel, which she never would have found on her own because it wasn't on HappyCow yet and wasn't on any English vegetarian/vegan website.

Despite this restaurant being five minutes from her hostel, The Traveler would have left Seoul without ever having found it. Which would have been a big shame because she had the most interesting food experience there, ordering what she thought was an ice cream sundae and ending up with shaved ice topped with beans, which is a traditional Korean dessert. The Traveler was so happy to have found the website and the café near her hostel, and was delighted to have a local friend who could show her around. And above all, she was elated to have found some vegan cake and coffee.

Lantern Festival
Seoul, Korea
2010

Blogs can be an excellent resource in your search for vegan places. There are two types of blogs you're likely to come across: bloggers based in the city you're visiting, and bloggers who've been there and reviewed it. Unfortunately Google has discontinued its blog-only search, but you can still find blogs if you go deep enough in Google's search results, by including "blog" in your search (e.g. "Greece vegan blog"), or sometimes by limiting the date range you're searching (if you're not sure how, check chapter 1). You can also limit search by language. If you find blog posts about the city that are dated from a while ago, don't forget to check the restaurants/stores mentioned are still open and in the same location!

Once you find bloggers who've visited (or are based in) the city, don't be afraid to email them directly, or leave a comment if you don't find their email address. (Tip: Their email is usually in the "About" or "Contact" section. Or try tweeting them. Most bloggers are regularly on Twitter and have Twitter buttons on their site which link to their Twitter profiles). Most bloggers love hearing from readers, and will be happy to help you with more information on the city. And again, if they're based there, they might even be willing to meet you for a coffee and some vegan cake! It would be nice if you treated them, though, as a "thank you" for the help they provided. Also, most bloggers love comments, so be sure to leave them a comment or send them a quick email or Tweet after your trip, letting them know you found their post(s) useful!

Drinks

Now that you've found information on restaurants, a quick note about drinks. If you're like me and you mainly drink cocktails, then you can probably skip this section as most (though not all) liquors are vegan. However, if you like beer and/or wine, Barnivore.com is an excellent resource for looking up which beers and wines are vegan. And liquors, too. It's easy to look on their database to see whether a given drink is vegan. However, you might want to download an app that uses the Barnivore database so that you can use it offline if you won't be able to use your data while on vacation. For this, I suggest iBarnivore (free, iOS), Vegaholic ($1.99, iOS), or VegeTipple ($1.99, Android).

Research Isn't Compulsory

That wraps up how to go about researching and finding vegetarian and vegan restaurants and drinks before your vacation. If you love planning your trips, poring over guidebooks and reading through Wikitravel guides, and deciding which sights to see, then you'll probably enjoy restaurant searching. If you're like me, and you refuse to read the Wikitravel guide until you're on the plane and loathe reading up on the destination before-hand, then you probably won't want to spend as much time reviewing restaurant listings. However, don't give up. Just try and think of it as an online adventure, a treasure hunt of sorts, where you're trying to find the buried treasure (somewhere in the vast pages of Google search results, there is one that actually tells you about vegetarian restaurants in that location!). But if you sit down at your computer and get all twitchy the minute you start thinking about exhaustively Googling and researching your destination, don't worry. The next section's for you.

* * *

Section 2:

Making Connections and Meeting New Friends.

• •

This section is all about how you can use the internet to find others who share your diet and lifestyle, and then use those connections to find plenty of food, as well as make new friends and have the trip of a lifetime. Because travel – and life – is always better when you make a connection. We're going to talk about how you can leverage the internet and your networks to find food recommendations – but also potential new friends in your destination.

Couchsurfing

Maybe you've heard of it. It sounds dangerous, and maybe a little gross. Staying on a stranger's sofa? "Yuck," you say. "Count me out!" Or maybe you're a super-adventurous type, and you think it sounds exciting. You're up for it, for sure. Imagine how much you could learn about their culture. Imagine the stories! No matter what you think of Couchsurfing, you may not have thought of it as a way to meet other vegetarians and vegans. But that's exactly what it is – and it's also an opportunity to find out about the local plant-based food scene from people in the know, even if Google leaves you in the lurch, with page after page of useless links.

Couchsurfing.org is a community project, which allows users (hosts) to offer up their sofas or spare rooms, and for other users who are visiting the area to request them. You register, put up some personal details, and then specify what you have available. You don't have to have a sofa or space to host someone in your house. You can just offer to meet people for coffee. It's a great tool to meet travelers in your town, and engage in cultural exchange, and it's also a fantastic tool for when you're traveling, even if the thought of staying on some random person's sofa gives you goosebumps. Couchsurfing is not just for staying on people's sofas, ladies and gents! It's about meeting people, learning about different cultures and – yes, really – it can also be about finding other vegans. So to find them, we need to do an advanced search. Again, you'll need your keyword list handy. We'll be searching people's profiles for those words!

First, if you don't have an account, you'll need to set one up. It's free to register, and free to sleep on these strangers' sofas (although it's nice to bring them a little gift if you can)! Once you've got an account set up, you'll need to search by filtering the city you're looking for. You can further select by types of "couch" available and male or female host, but at this point just filter by city – we're just looking for people to make friends with, rather than find a place to sleep! (If you want to use Couchsurfing to find a place to stay, we'll cover that in Section 4.)

The most important bit for our purposes is in the advanced search options: we want to do a keyword search, using our keywords from our original list like vegan, vegetarian etc. You'll find people who have mentioned these words in their profiles. IMPORTANT: it's really critical to read each individual profile! What we're doing here is just a keyword search to find mentions of the words, which does NOT mean that the person is a vegan or vegetarian or into healthy eating. Sometimes you will find that they've actually said something like "I'm a dedicated carnivore who hates meatless food with a passion." And they've turned up in your search for the word "meatless." That's why it's really important to read their profile – you don't want to be messaging them asking for tips on the best vegetarian restaurants!

Let's say you've found a few people who mention your keywords in their profile and you've read their profiles to check they are actually veggie or interested in vegetarian or vegan food… Now the fun bit starts! First off, if you haven't set up your own profile, you should do so now, before you contact anyone. If you've got a blank profile, people will be less likely to respond. Couchsurfing may consist of meeting relative strangers or letting them stay with you, but people still want to know a bit about you first! Send a message to the people you've found and tell them you're interested in meeting them for coffee, and learning more about where to find healthy/ meat-free/vegan options in the city. Mention something about their profile to show you've actually read it and are not just spamming them with a message. It helps if you make a personal connection, especially if you find a common interest in addition to diet and lifestyle (like you both really love heavy metal, or you're both into skateboarding).

Couchsurfing has bailed me out of trouble many a time, so I strongly advise you to use it if you run into any difficult situations as well, for example if you aren't able to find any vegetarian restaurants or places with veg options. If you can find someone on Couchsurfing, they can probably help you out!

Here are a few of the many ways Couchsurfing has saved me:

Croatia, 2009

I did my homework and my planning and found the one vegetarian restaurant in Dubrovnik at the time (which I subsequently ended up visiting every single day of the week I was there, and sampling everything vegan on the menu, as well as making good friends with the owner, who gave me a lot of free muffins). However, my plane landed on a Sunday evening, the one day the restaurant was closed. I knew I'd be too tired to want to wander around trying to find a supermarket (and the B&B I was staying in didn't have a kitchen). I messaged a vegan on Couchsurfing who immediately told me where I could get a cheeseless pizza. I was so glad I'd sent that message, because when I landed I discovered 95% of restaurants were fish restaurants and if I hadn't had the address of the pizza place I might have gone dinner-less, or had a dinner of beans from a can (just like one of the horror stories).

Argentina, 2010

I was nearly stranded without a place to stay over Christmas. Everywhere I turned was booked up, even though I was in the huge metropolis of Buenos Aires. I couldn't find a single hostel or decently priced hotel – the only things that seemed to be available were ridiculously overpriced. In an act of desperation, I messaged a seemingly friendly vegetarian girl asking to stay the next day. And she said yes! I ended up in a really amazing flat with my own en-suite bathroom, and we had a lot of fun cooking a vegan dinner together and discussing veganism, as she was interested in going vegan.

Chile, 2010

I didn't know a soul in Santiago and after a couple of months of traveling was starting to get lonely. I messaged a vegan who not only took me out for a fun night on the town, but also gave me a long list of suggested vegan restaurants and even a store to visit.

Santa Lucia Park
Santiago, Chile
2010

Meetup

If you haven't checked out Meetup.com yet, do so now. It's an amazing resource for finding like-minded individuals in your area, and joining activities geared toward your area of interest! Simply search your city, and interest areas (like blogging, veganism, knitting and more). It's also a fantastic place to find people with shared interests in the city you're visiting. You could use it to find people who share your love of softball and who want to go for a game, but in our case we're going to use it to find fellow plant eaters.

You can set a city and the number of miles, so set it to something like "within 10 miles of XXX [city you will be visiting]". Next, enter your search terms – pick one of the words from your keyword list. If there's a vegetarian Meetup group in that city, then great – sign up! It's free to create an account on Meetup.com, and join different groups.

You'll likely need to provide a little information about yourself, like why you want to join the group. Sometimes you are able to join a group with the click of a button and sometimes the administrator of the group needs to approve your application. This will usually only take a day or so.

Once you've signed up and joined the group or been approved, have a look and see if they're planning a Meetup (like visiting a veggie restaurant, having a picnic, or another activity) while you're in the area! You'll need to RSVP so that the organizers know you're attending. In the case of smaller venues, they may have a limit on the number of people who can attend. If you are put on the Waitlist because all the spots at the venue are taken, keep checking back because if anyone changes their RSVP from "yes" to "no" the people on the Waitlist will be given a spot at the Meetup.

Meetups are free to attend unless otherwise noted on the Meetup page, but if it's a meal or drinks, you'll be expected to pay your part of the tab, of course. If they're not holding an official group event, but you want to meet people, you can post in the members' area of the group and see if anyone is up for meeting unofficially. Or you can suggest an event to the organizer. (Depending on the group settings, there is sometimes an option to suggest an event.) Or if you're struggling to figure out where you should go in the city, you can write a message in the forum/members' area asking for suggestions!

And like I said, it's all about making a connection, and most people are really keen to help out a fellow vegan/vegetarian. When I was visiting Beijing, I signed up to the Beijing vegan meet up and RSVP'd to attend one of the dinners – which just happened to be the week I was there! Lucky! Unfortunately, I got a horrible flu and was bedridden much of the week in the hostel. It was pretty miserable for a couple of days, until I sent the Meetup organizer a message saying I wouldn't be able to attend the dinner as I was so ill. She replied right away, saying how sorry she was that I was sick, and recommending a Chinese herbal tea that I could get in any drugstore. Armed with her recommendation, I went the drugstore around the corner the very next morning, and felt better after my very first cup. Unfortunately I didn't improve in time for the Meetup, but the tea saved my trip, because I nearly ended up missing the Forbidden City due to my illness but recovered just in time to get out of the hostel and see the sights!

Forums

Forums are another great resource for finding out about restaurants and for connecting with locals. Check out the forums on The Post Punk

Kitchen [http://forum.theppk.com/] and The Vegan Forum [http://www.veganforum.com/].

If you haven't been on a forum before, it's normally arranged into boards. If the forum were a neighborhood, the boards would be the houses. Each board has a theme. For example, you might have Europe, North America and Australia as boards. Then within each board, you have a thread. This is like a room in a house, and it's where you'll find all the people at the forum-party. These are the topics. You can start a new thread, or respond to an old one. It's considered polite to have a search through the archives before starting a thread, to make sure one doesn't already exist. Hey, if you were throwing a party, and someone was already hosting one in another room in the same house, it would be a bit rude to start an entirely new party! If you search and you do come across a thread, but it's a couple of years old, feel free to bring it back to life by commenting on the thread. Don't worry, even though it's old, people will still see it. Your comment will "bump" the thread – that means it will become visible again at the top of the board, and everyone accessing the board will see it as soon as they click on the board. If you search and don't come across anything, start your own new thread. You can post where you're going and see if anyone else has been there on vacation and has recommendations, and you can also try and connect with local veggies. Who knows, a group of locals might even be hosting a meet soon in the city you're visiting, or they might be willing to meet up with you!

Social Networks

Maybe someone you are connected with on Facebook or Twitter or Instagram has been to (or is from!) the place you're visiting, and you don't even realize. Or perhaps they know someone who has. It's always worth posting on Facebook or Twitter that you're going there, and asking whether anyone has any recommendations. Even if they don't, they might be able to put you in touch with someone who does. A Facebook friend who I don't know very well recently posted she is going to Berlin and Austria, and was inundated with suggestions of what to do and where to eat. I don't speak to her very frequently (the last time we spoke was probably a year ago), but it came up in my feed so I added a few suggestions too, along with a dozen other people. You can also try a vegetarian and vegan-specific network like Volentia, which is sort of like Facebook for the veg community.

On Facebook, there's an extremely helpful group called Vegan Travel (just search for it and request to join) where you can post all your vegan travel questions. There are thousands of members so likely someone in there has been to the place you are visiting and can help!

On Twitter, try adding hashtags to your tweet so people can find you more easily. For example, #vegantravel, or you can be more specific like #veganberlin. Before posting, try checking on the search tool if anyone else has been tweeting with that hashtag recently. It will give you an idea of how popular and active the hashtag is. You might also find some useful tweets about the city that people have sent with that hashtag!

Asking People

Good old-fashioned offline conversations are another great way to make connections and find out about places to go. Reach out to vegetarians and vegans you know in your hometown. (If you don't know any, try looking at Meetup and Couchsurfing to see if there are any local groups to connect with!) See if they've been to the place you're visiting, or if they know anyone who has, and ask for recommendations. Likewise, see if they have any contacts who live there. They might just have some great suggestions, or be able to put you in touch with locals, who, by the way, are more likely to want to advise you and meet up with you if you're a friend of a friend. Don't you find a mutual connection always serves as a "reference" and that you're more likely to want to help out someone connected to you, however distantly? As humans, we're wired to behave like this. With so much sensory information coming in, we implicitly trust our connections, and by extension, their connections.

You can also try to get some recommendations through word of mouth once you're actually there. Just go to the vegan restaurants and health food stores you've discovered through your online research and ask them for suggestions of other places to go. They might be able to tell you about new places that have opened up recently, which aren't even listed online yet, but which they've heard about, thanks to their local connections and – you guessed it – good old-fashioned word of mouth!

* * *

Section 3:

What to Do With Your List.

· ·

Okay, so you've made your list. You've exhausted the internet, and asked every great-aunt and friend-of-a-friend you can think of if they've been to your destination. You've searched every word you can think of, you've looked at Google search results to approximately page 5823. You've asked for advice on every forum and social network you're a member of (you even joined some new ones!). You've got a nice fat list of restaurants to visit. But now what do you do? How do you keep track of everything?

Make a Folder or Booklet

My suggestion is to make yourself a booklet or folder with the most important information. You can simply print it all off as separate web pages from HappyCow/Meetup/etc, and put it in a big folder to take with you, alongside your plane tickets and hotel reservations. If you want to save particular articles, you can print those off – or, my favorite option, save them to an app for offline use, like Evernote or Pocket. At the end of this book you'll find a list of my favorite apps to download. Evernote is a notebook app, which allows you to create docs, save pieces of text and quotes, and keep them super organized into different folders. I'm not into filing systems, but people I know who love filing and organizing are absolutely in love with their Evernote. One downside is you can no longer view them offline unless you upgrade to a (paid) premium account. My preferred app is Pocket, which allows you to save whole web pages for offline viewing – for free. You can also use Pinterest to create a visual board for your trip and Pin webpages that you find and want to save – for example restaurants, hotels, and attractions.

Key information I'd suggest including:

- Each restaurant, with name, address, opening times, phone number and email.

- Translations of key words and phrases.

- List of traditional local foods that you can likely eat.

Putting Your Information Together: Google Maps

Okay, so you've got all your information together now for your folder or booklet, including your list of restaurants, translations, and local foods. But what if you don't want to waste paper and ink? What about going digital? I'd definitely recommend creating your own Google map if you're traveling within your country and can use the internet on your phone without being charged exorbitant fees, or if money is no object and you don't mind using your phone abroad, or if you're going to get a local SIM card that allows you to use data at a decent price. (This is great if you're going to be somewhere for a bit longer term.) If you're anything like me, you basically can't find your way around without your map on your phone and your GPS. You probably follow that little blue dot mindlessly around, not even stopping to look up – if it tried to walk you straight through a solid building, you probably would!

But what if you're going to be abroad and not be able to use the search function on maps? You can save the map for offline use – and even "star" restaurants, attractions, and other places of interest for offline. Your phone will let you use the map (including the lifesaving little blue dot which shows you where you are!) even when you aren't connected to the internet. This is the most amazing thing ever when you're abroad and you've had to turn off your data. It means that suddenly, you can have a map that shows you where you are at any time. No more getting lost in strange cities! Unfortunately it can't give directions, or use the compass (so you can't see which way you're facing), unless you're connected to the internet.

While you can't search for directions on the go without an internet connection, you can connect your phone to the internet, search for directions, go offline, and then follow those directions, as long as you don't restart your phone at any point while you are en route. (Note: This works on iPhones but is not enabled on Android at the time of writing – however, Google have said they plan to release an offline map feature on Android by the end of 2015.) So try entering your destination while connected to internet in the hotel in the morning, or on free Wi-Fi found in a café where you get your morning/mid-afternoon coffee, and then going offline and following said map.

To save a map for offline use on your phone, pull up a map of the city. Zoom out until you have as much of the city (and surrounding areas) on your screen as possible. Google will only save the area shown on the screen for offline, so make sure to get in as much as possible. However, bear in mind it can only save 50km by 50km at a time, so if the map you want to save is too big you may want to do a few saves, zooming in on different parts of the map. Oh, and if Google gives you an error ('cannot save') it's probably because you're zoomed too far out (like trying to save an entire county!) and it's too much information for Google to handle. Zoom in a little, and try again. Depending on how big the city is, you might be able to save the entire city in one go, or you might need to save different areas of the city at a time, depending on where you're planning to go and how much of the map you need. ⟶

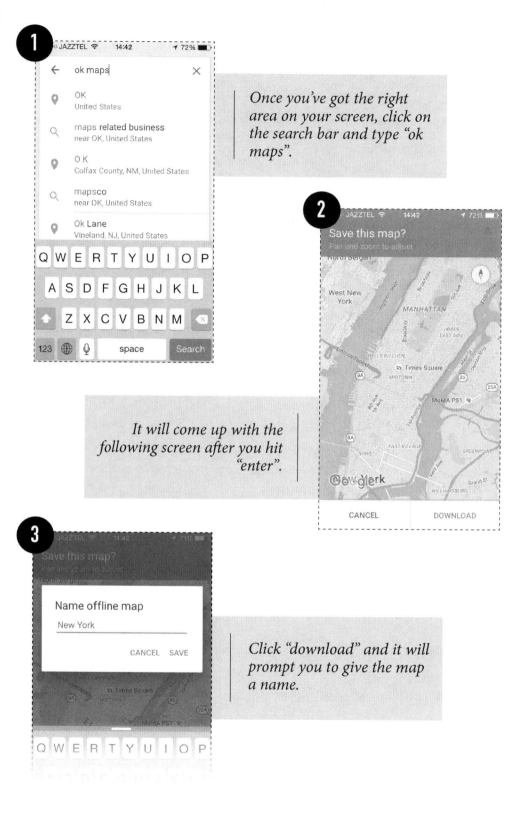

1

← ok maps ✕

◉ OK
United States

🔍 maps **related business**
near OK, United States

◉ O K
Colfax County, NM, United States

🔍 **mapsco**
near OK, United States

◉ Ok **Lane**
Vineland, NJ, United States

Once you've got the right area on your screen, click on the search bar and type "ok maps".

2

Save this map?
Pan and zoom to adjust

CANCEL   DOWNLOAD

It will come up with the following screen after you hit "enter".

3

Name offline map

New York

CANCEL   SAVE

Click "download" and it will prompt you to give the map a name.

4

Saving ✕

Once you've named the map and clicked "save" you will get a screen telling you the map is saving.

5

Candle 79

Candle 79
4.5 ★★★★★ (159) · £££ · Route

To star a place, drop a pin where you want to go. (To drop a pin, simply hold your finger on the location for a few seconds, and a pin will drop), then click "favorites" and it will be starred. Or, look up a restaurant, hotel, or attraction and once this screen comes up, click on the name of the restaurant:

6

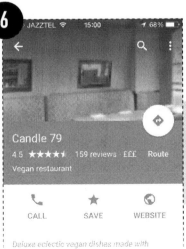

Candle 79
4.5 ★★★★★ 159 reviews · £££ Route
Vegan restaurant

CALL   SAVE   WEBSITE

Deluxe eclectic vegan dishes made with organic produce & served in elegant surroundings.

On the next screen, click on the star button:

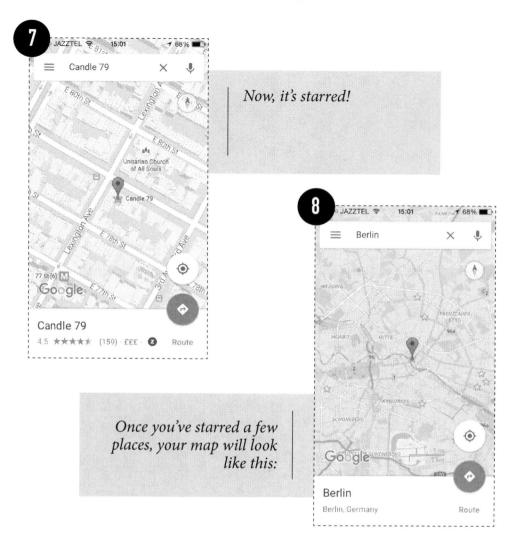

Now, it's starred!

Once you've starred a few places, your map will look like this:

You can see the stars on our map later, even when you're offline. Sadly, you won't be able to search for individual places or restaurants and directions when you're offline, so it's important to save the map and star any special places before you're cut off from Wi-Fi! You can do this before your trip, or if you have Wi-Fi in your hotel/hostel/apartment, save it in the morning before you go out for the day.

Or you could go the really old-fashioned route, and print out some paper maps! I find the easiest way to do this is to print out some maps showing each restaurant/store you want to go to, ideally zoomed in a bit on the local area so you can see the nearest streets. Then, once you reach your destination, get one of those paper fold-out maps of the city they give away free at most hostels, hotels and airports. Take a pen, and using the paper maps you printed out before, locate each restaurant on the map and mark it in pen, with the name. That way, when you're wandering around looking at the sights, you'll be able to look at your map, spot your location on the map, and see which restaurants are nearest.

A final note: Plan out your first meal once you arrive carefully – you may be really hungry and tired when you get off the plane. I suggest using HappyCow/Google maps to find the restaurant closest to your apartment/hotel/hostel/Couchsurfing host, check they're open, and make a Google map with directions from the place you're staying to that restaurant. Then, when you arrive bedraggled off the plane, you can go check into your hotel, take a quick shower if needed, and go straight to that restaurant when it's time for lunch/dinner. If you don't find anything within walking distance, find out what the nearest metro station is, and locate a restaurant that's easy to get to via metro. Trust me, when you first arrive and are jetlagged, the last thing you want to be doing is wandering around, trying to find a restaurant that's open, not really sure where you're going or if you're in a safe area, in the dark.

Likewise, plan your last meal – if your flight leaves at an awkward time, you might want to stock up on food the night before, or earlier in the day before your flight, so you have some goodies to take with you on the plane and to tide you over before and during your flight.

Looking Up Opening Times and Addresses

Want a sure way to get screwed, go hungry and get in a massive fight with your travel companions? No? Well then you better double-check the location and hours of the restaurants on your list. Don't just go trust HappyCow, or even Google. I know because of personal experience with my now ex, a holiday that could have gone very wrong because of my lack of checking out opening times!

It was our very first holiday together as a couple.

We'd only been together a few months, and this was a huge test of our relationship. I know that travel can bring out the best and worst in a person, and so we knew going into it that this would be one of our first — and most important — tests as a couple. It would make or break us. Imagine my dismay when, after getting off the flight and getting the bus into town, we found ourselves, stomachs growling, wandering through the sunbaked streets of Bratislava, Slovakia in search of an elusive vegan restaurant that was not where it said it would be. Eventually, over an hour into our wanderings, we decided we had to stop and call the restaurant, and upon going to their website to search for the number, discovered that the restaurant was not where HappyCow or Google said it would be. It had moved, and no one had reported it to HappyCow yet, which relies on its users for reviews and updates. Nor had Google updated it on Maps or on their search page results. Luckily, we were able to quickly locate another vegan-friendly restaurant nearby that I had on my list of places, and go there before our rumbling stomachs caused a fight — and ruined our weekend.

So, what should you do to prevent dehydrating yourself walking around in the baking hot sun for an hour or more looking for a restaurant that may have moved? Start with your list of restaurants and stores, and look up, at minimum, the opening days and hours (noting down in particular any days each restaurant is shut, or days it closes early) and the address. If you think you may want to call them once there, write down the phone numbers, too. You can even email in advance and verify the times they're open, and the days you're going. It's also a good idea to make sure things aren't closed because of holidays, especially if you're going over traditional holidays (Christmas, New Year's, Chinese New Year, etc.) or times when a lot of the local population is away and may close restaurants temporarily. Be prepared to be surprised by local holidays you didn't even know existed.

For example, one year during our summer holidays in Sicily, we discovered that everyone else in Sicily was on holiday, too. Pretty much the whole island (like much of Italy) was closed for August. Just about everyone had headed off on their own holidays, making the city a ghost town. Restaurant after restaurant I'd eagerly anticipated visiting was shut, until we discovered that every single vegetarian restaurant I had on my list was shut. Luckily, we didn't starve – but I did learn an important lesson: to check local holidays!

Look up any traditional holidays occurring during the time you're visiting, or check individual restaurants' sites, Twitter, or Facebook. (Twitter and Facebook are often the best places to check because they are updated frequently and many restaurant owners post when they're about to close for holidays.) Not all restaurants do post notices, though, so don't assume they will. (If in doubt, or you know a local holiday is coming up, always email or call.)

If you've created a folder or Evernote file, note down restaurant opening times and up-to-date addresses.

Don't Starve Just Because It's Sunday

Okay, so now you should have a list of restaurants, and also their opening times (and addresses). Have you started to notice any trends in days when restaurants are closed? In many places, there's a day when most restaurants are closed. It's commonly Sunday or Monday. If you're in a place where there's a day like this, you might find it hard to eat on that day, so it's important to note which restaurants are open that day. You can check your list by going through each restaurant individually, or you can use an app. Doodle isn't made for this purpose at all, but it fits the bill. If you're not familiar with Doodle, it's a really cool free scheduling app, which helps you pick a time for a group of people to meet based on everyone's availability. You put in some details about the event plus days and times, and people go in and write down their names and whether or not they can come at those times – and Doodle tells you which day is most popular. Handy if your friends, like mine, are so busy you can't even find a day to go for a drink together! We're going to use it to visually see when restaurants are open. It will look like this, with green ticks representing the restaurant being open, and red "Xs" that it's closed.

To make one, you simply start by choosing dates from a calendar. In our example, we'll assume you are visiting Barcelona for the weekend, from late morning Friday until Sunday afternoon.

7 participants	November 2015 Fri 13		Sat 14			Sun 15	
	Friday Lunch	Friday Dinner	Saturday breakfast	Saturday Lunch	Saturday Dinner	Sunday breakfast	Sunday lunch
Sesamo		✓			✓		
Teresa Carles	✓	✓	✓	✓	✓	✓	✓
Rizoma		✓			✓		
Rasoterra	✓	✓		✓	✓		✓
Juicy Jones	✓	✓	✓	✓		✓	✓
Cat Bar		✓			✓		
Dolce Pizza y los Ve	✓	✓		✓	✓		✓
Your name	☐	☐	☐	☐	☐	☐	☐
	4	7	2	4	7	2	4

Go to Doodle's homepage [http://doodle.com] and click on "schedule event" (it's free!). It will ask you to fill out the name of the event and your email address (don't worry, Doodle don't spam you):

Next, it will ask you to choose the dates – in this example, we'll choose the days you will be in Barcelona:

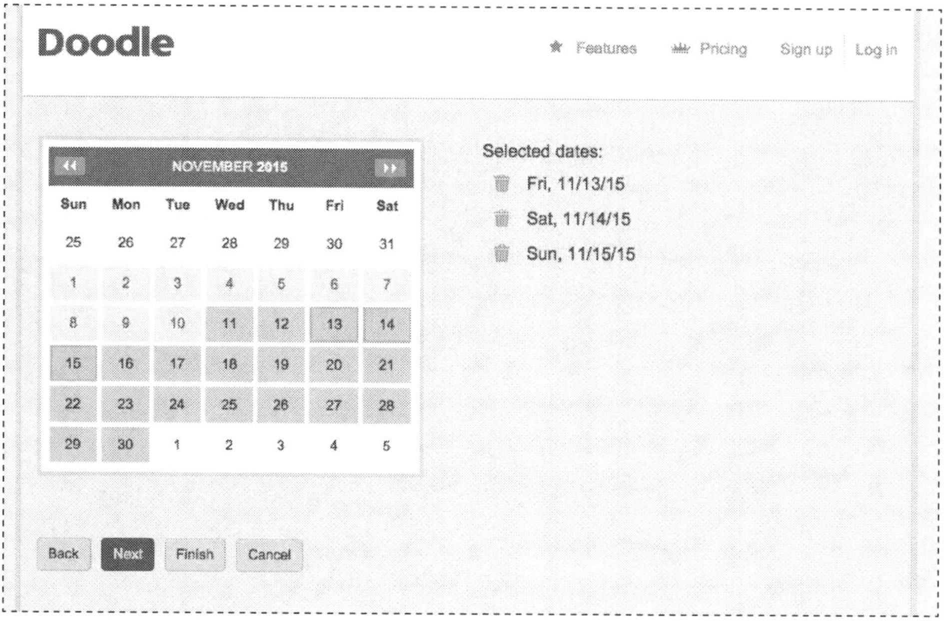

The next screen will ask you to choose times. I'd suggest choosing mealtimes for each day:

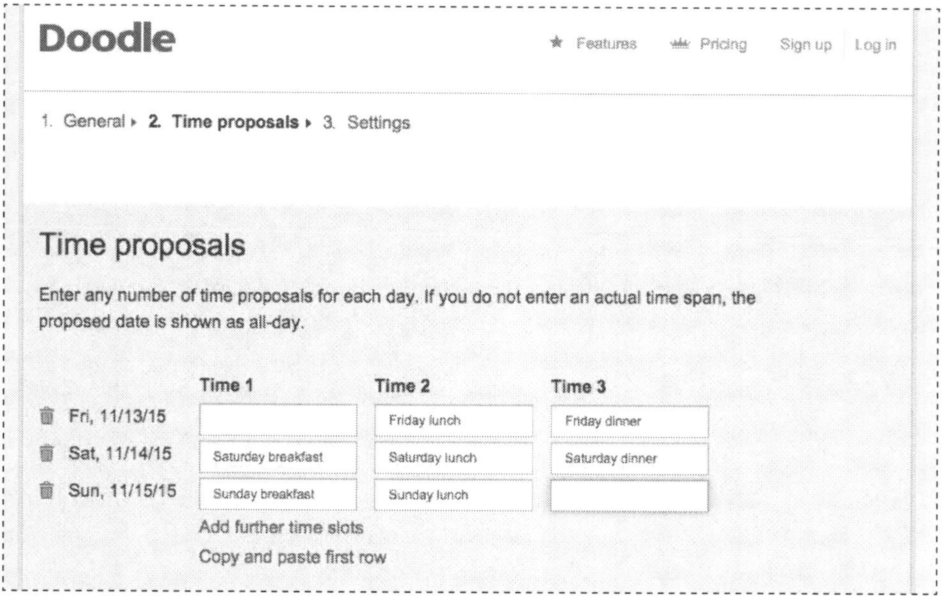

After this, you can select the basic poll option:

After you select the basic poll option, you'll receive a "participation link" to the poll on the next screen (and in your e-mail). Go to the participation link, and you'll be given the option to put your name in and participate in the poll. Here, you'll put the name of each restaurant and tick each time of day that they're open. For example, Sesamo in Barcelona is open from 8pm to midnight every day except Monday, so we will put Sesamo and tick "Friday dinner" and "Saturday dinner," then click the "save" button:

We'll need to go back to the poll and complete for each restaurant on our list. We'll end up with the poll results from the first screenshot:

Doodle ★ Features 👑 P

Table view

7 participants	Friday Lunch	Friday Dinner	Saturday breakfast	Saturday Lunch	Saturday Dinner	Sunday breakfast	Sunday lunch
Sesamo		✓			✓		
Teresa Carles	✓	✓	✓	✓	✓	✓	✓
Rizoma		✓			✓		
Rasoterra	✓	✓		✓	✓		✓
Juicy Jones	✓	✓	✓	✓	✓	✓	✓
Cat Bar		✓			✓		
Dolce Pizza y los Ve	✓	✓		✓	✓		✓
Your name	☐	☐	☐	☐	☐	☐	☐
	4	7	2	4	7	2	4

November 2015 — Fri 13 · Sat 14 · Sun 15

For example, this shows me that if we're looking for a place for breakfast Sunday, we should choose Teresa Carles or Juicy Jones, as all the other restaurants are closed for breakfast.

Translations

Okay, you're thinking, that's all well and good, but what the hell am I supposed to do if I search, and search, and search and can't find any vegan restaurants? What if I've exhausted all the resources, and I still can't find anything? Well first of all, you might want to consider a self-catered option. If you've got your own kitchen, you've got a lot more flexibility, and you won't need to worry about whether or not you can find restaurants that cater to your dietary needs. However, you probably still want to be able to eat out. You're on holiday, after all, you don't want to be slaving away in the kitchen all day!

This is where the internet comes in handy yet again. (We should all say a massive thank you to the internet for its existence now, and for making our lives so much easier in so many ways!) Now, instead of asking the internet about vegetarian or vegan restaurants in your destination, we'll be looking up how to say vegetarian/vegan (and a few other words) in the local language, local traditions, and local traditional foods which you can eat.

Did you know that there's a special magic word in Thai ("jay") that you can say that will pretty much guarantee you vegan food in any restaurant? Or that this word ("jay") and a similar word ("chay") can be used in Laos ("jay"), Vietnam ("chay"), and Cambodia ("chay")?

Thanks to the internet, we can find out about local traditions and words in other languages without ever leaving our sofa or meeting someone from that country.

First things first, you may want to consider getting a Vegan Passport. These are little books, made to fit easily in a handbag or backpack, which you're meant to hand to your server in a restaurant. They explain, in 85 languages, that you're vegan, and what you do and don't eat.

The Vegan Passport is in fact a little controversial, because they go into a lot of detail, not just about what vegans do and don't eat, but about the ethics of being vegan, which some people think could be off-putting to the person you hand it to. Personally, I think they're a good backup option, and I don't think they'd necessarily put the person reading it off veganism, but I think it contains far too much information for what's meant to be a relatively short interaction. (No one's going to read the whole thing, most will skim at best). That aside, it might not be a bad option to keep one in your bag or pocket, at least as a safety net. Some people even cover up the ethics explanation bit with a bit of tape – however I find this a little risky when done in languages you really can't comprehend. You might just be covering highly crucial details of what you don't eat that the server needs to communicate to the chef.

If you are planning on shopping in supermarkets or health food stores and want to be able to translate ingredients lists, in Europe you've now got the option of buying the European Vegan Zine, which contains translations of common animal ingredients, and E numbers (additives), so you can easily skim ingredients lists in any European language.

If you don't want to buy a Vegan Passport, or you have other dietary requirements, you can make your own list of translations in the local language and bring these with you, or put them in your folder or booklet.

Some phrases you may want to translate:

- I am vegan.

- I am vegetarian.

- I do not eat meat, chicken or pork.

- I do not eat fish.

- I do not eat eggs.

- I do not drink milk, eat butter or cheese, or consume dairy products.

- I do not consume honey.

- I do not eat ghee.

- Is there chicken/beef/pork/fish stock in this?

- Is there oyster sauce in this?

- Is there fish sauce in this?

- Is there shrimp paste in this?

- Is there lard in this?

Where should you get your translations? Well, Google Translate does a fairly decent job with simple words and phrases, but the more complicated your phrases get, the more it may struggle. Of course, you won't know whether the translation's perfect or not until you try it. So you should probably check your translations against a few sites, and if you know anyone who speaks the language, ask them for help! If you found any new contacts via Couchsurfing, you can also ask them, or post some questions on your Twitter, Facebook or other social network and see if any of your friends or their friends speak the language and can help out. You never know who might be following you and what languages they speak!

Eating Like a Local

It's also worth having a look at local traditions, and finding out if there are any holidays or religious traditions that encourage veganism or vegetarianism. Normally, you'll find that these are religious, for example Eastern Orthodox Lent (for which many followers go vegetarian) or the Buddhist Vegetarian Festival in Thailand. Read up on the local religions and any festivals or holidays, and see whether any of them involve vegetarianism.

Did you know, for example, that in Ethiopia there's a time of year and certain days of the week when you can expect a large portion of the population to be eating vegan, and therefore vegan food is a lot easier to come by? (Lent, Wednesdays and Fridays)

Or that in Romania and Russia a large portion of the population eats mainly vegan during Lent and prior to Christmas?

Finally, read up on local foods and find out whether any traditional dishes look like they're accidentally vegan or vegetarian (or easy to modify). For example, quite often in Italy marinara pizza is available which is simply a pizza with tomato sauce and garlic with no cheese. (This is a very traditional, very basic pizza marinara.) In Greece, there are lots of accidentally vegan dishes, like the hummus-esque "fava," which is a bean purée made from yellow split peas. You might just discover a new favorite dish to make when you get home!

The best way to find these sorts of dishes is to go back to your list of words to Google, but expand your search to encompass an entire region or country instead of the city, and maybe add on "dishes" or "foods" into your search, for example:

- Vegan Greek dishes
- Vegetarian traditional Italian foods

* * *

Section 4:

Where to Stay & How to Choose.

Now that we've got our list of restaurants, our translations of phrases, and information on local foods that are usually vegan, we're ready to choose where to stay! In this section, we'll be discussing how to use your list of restaurants to pick the most vegan-friendly area to stay. Then, we'll discuss the pros and cons of different accommodation options, including hotels, B&Bs and guesthouses, hostels, Couchsurfing, Airbnb, housesitting, Vegvisits, and renting a holiday apartment.

Find a Vegan-Friendly Area

When choosing a place to stay on holiday, people's brains typically run through a laundry list of their own personal priorities. Yours might include cost, location, proximity to the airport or public transit, cleanliness, whether it has Wi-Fi, if it has a pool, atmosphere, whether it's quiet or loud, safety, and more. You may also want to consider its vegetarian- and vegan-friendliness. If it serves breakfast, do they have a vegan option? Is there a fridge in the room for you to store snacks or soy milk? If it's a hostel, does it have a kitchen so you could cook? Is it close to vegetarian restaurants? We're going to talk about a variety of different options of where to stay, as well as what questions you should be asking. Before we do that, though, I just want to talk in really general terms about how to choose a location/neighborhood. Now, putting all other considerations aside (hey, keep your list of priorities, just put your notebook down for a second), we're going to think just about how to choose a vegan-friendly location.

Have a look on HappyCow (using the map feature, go to the city you're going to and then pull up the map of the city, it will look something like this):

And/or on Google (by Googling "vegetarian restaurants" or "vegan restaurants" and pulling up the ¬map). See where the greatest concentration of vegetarian restaurants are (hint: normally in the city center, surrounding a university, or in an area known for counterculture), and then look for places to stay in that vicinity. Alternatively, you might want to consider places which are close to a restaurant with vegan breakfast/brunch options, or places near a restaurant that you want to go to for dinner, or near a health food store if you're getting somewhere with a kitchen and plan to cook. (Or if you're like one of my friends, look for a place which has a freezer near a store selling vegan ice cream!)

Once you've located a neighborhood you want to stay in, you now have a plethora of different options: hotel, hostel, Airbnb, Couchsurfing, B&B, renting an apartment, canoe (okay, maybe not the last one… although you can stay in a boat hostel in Stockholm). We're going to break each one down into pros and cons (with relation to vegetarian-friendliness) as well as consider which options are best (depending on your situation and city) plus what questions you should ask.

Hotels

This might be (or at least it used to be) the standard option for many travelers, but it's my least favorite. Not just because chain hotels tend to be standardized and soulless, but because they don't afford many options for us. They usually don't have kitchens or sometimes even fridges (unless you upgrade to a suite), and if they offer one of those standard hotel breakfast buffets, they probably won't have loads of vegan options laid out. If you're going to book a hotel, make sure you have some vegan breakfast options in the local vicinity, have checked with the hotel that they can accommodate you at breakfast, or have a plan of what you can eat in the room. For example, bring some quick-cook oatmeal and make it with the tea kettle/coffeemaker in your room, or have fruit for breakfast. For recipes to make in a coffeemaker, check Section 7. Alternatively, buy cereal and some single-serving sized UHT soymilk cartons – that's the kind that you can leave out of the fridge. Some hotels are getting better at stocking soy milk, or will be willing to get some in if you ask in advance, so you might be able to have a coffee and cereal.

You can check out apartment hotels, which are hotels consisting of mini apartments, and can be an inexpensive option in some cities.

On the plus side, if you stay in a really posh, five-star hotel, they will almost certainly cater to your needs and even if their restaurant doesn't have any vegan options on the menu, they will very likely make something for you on request.

My favorite place to book a hotel is Hotels.com, because they offer an excellent reward system – for every ten nights you book through their website, you get one night free! If you're traveling last minute, though, you might want to try Lastminute.com or Hotel Tonight (a free app).

B&Bs and Guesthouses

B&Bs can be a really great option, if you find one that's willing to make you a vegetarian or vegan breakfast. You can even find some vegetarian and vegan B&Bs, which are excellent, because not only will you be fed a morning meal without having to worry about it, you can probably even get tips from the B&B owner about nearby restaurants with vegetarian and vegan dishes! Some guesthouses serve breakfast and also have the option of buying dinner, which makes your life even easier, because you can always go back to the guesthouse if you can't find any vegan options. This is great in places that are a bit more remote.

Vegan breakfasts and brunches can be difficult to find, particularly since a lot of vegetarian restaurants don't open until lunchtime. You're probably going to be doing a lot of walking and sightseeing so it's important to start the day off right with a hearty breakfast! Have a look and see if there are any vegetarian or vegan B&Bs, but if there aren't, don't give up. A lot of B&Bs are willing to make vegan breakfasts, so just ask before booking and see if they will accommodate you!

For example, I once stayed in a B&B in a rural part of the Isle of Wight. Now, this B&B was not only extremely beautiful, but they also did us an absolutely fantastic vegan breakfast. And it wasn't advertised on their site. My friend just emailed and asked if they could do us a vegan breakfast – the reply was that the owner was vegetarian herself, and always had vegan sausages on hand. In the end, our multi-course breakfast included a fruit course, followed by cereal and soy yogurt course, followed by a full English fry-up.

Hostels

Hostels aren't just a budget-friendly option good for your wallet, they're also good for vegans! If you're not into sharing space with others, don't worry, most hostels have private rooms these days, and some have en-suite options too, if you want your own bathroom. Most hostels have kitchen facilities that are free for use, and which come equipped with pots, pans and even, sometimes, basic ingredients (oils, salt and pepper, even some spices). You might have to fight through a line in order to get your turn cooking, though.

The best places to look for hostels are Hostel World and Hostel Bookers, both of which will mark whether a hostel has kitchen facilities or not. Or just email the hostel and ask before booking! Not only will having a kitchen mean you don't have to worry so much about finding food – you can always cook up something quick if needed (check out the recipes section for some ideas) – but it also means you can save some money while you're at it! Hostels tend to attract alternative types, and I've met many other vegetarians and vegans in hostels, so you might just meet some fellow vegans who can recommend places to eat.

When you check in to the hostel, ask about nearby grocery stories (people working at hostels are used to getting asked this, and will normally provide you with a free map with the nearby bus stops, supermarkets, and attractions marked down), and go pick up a few things to make sure you've got some snacks (like fruit, nuts, etc.) as well as some breakfast options (grab some cereal or oats and non-dairy milk, if they have it at the grocery; if not check for a health food store). Most hostels with kitchen facilities will let you keep food in the fridge too – just make sure you write your name on it in marker pen, or someone may eat it!

Couchsurfing

I mentioned Couchsurfing as a way of finding other vegans and asking for advice, but it's also obviously a good option for finding places to stay (since that's what it was built for!). The concept of Couchsurfing is that you can find a sofa to stay on – free – just about anywhere, making travel more practical, but also allowing you to engage in cultural exchange. Instead of staying in a run-of-the-mill hotel, and never speaking to any locals, you can sleep in their house and learn about new cultures, as well as make new friends. Actually a lot of Couchsurfers are expats, so you may find that the "local" you're staying with isn't so local.

Couchsurfing isn't just couches (despite the name): you might find yourself staying in a spare room, or on the floor. Usually this is noted in the host's profile, so you know what you're getting. Keep in mind Couchsurfing is about building community and learning about other cultures, and Couchsurfers do not appreciate it if you are just looking for a free place to crash, and not interested in learning about new cultures.

It's considered polite to return the favor – not necessarily by hosting the people who hosted you, but by becoming a host yourself when you return home, or at the very least offering up your availability to take people passing through your city for coffee. (You can set on your profile what sort of availability you have – couch, if you've got somewhere for people to crash, or just coffee, if you don't have the capacity/don't want someone to stay in your house, but are willing to meet people and show them around.)

As we spoke about previously, you can use the keyword search in Couchsurfing to find other vegans and vegetarians. If you're staying with someone, you might want to find someone who's vegetarian or vegan, so you know they'll be able to recommend eateries to you and that they'll have vegetarian or vegan food in the house. If you don't mind, or can't find a vegan or vegetarian to stay with, you should still mention your dietary requirements to your host before you arrive (and be explicit about what it means, in case they aren't familiar with the concept or the English word), lest they prepare their grandmother's favorite lamb stew and try to feed you spoonfuls of it the moment you walk in the door.

A note on safety: Before Couchsurfing, read up a bit on safety concerns and make sure you know what you're getting yourself into. There have been reports of rape, assault and attacks, although there aren't many in comparison to the volume of Couchsurfing going on. Make sure you take precautions to protect yourself. Read reviews on the host, think about whether or not you want to stay with a single male/female, a couple, or a group, and consider what you'd do in case something bad did happen. Never, ever stay somewhere if you feel uncomfortable once you've met the person/set foot in their house. Always have the number/address of a hostel as a backup, and know how to get yourself there should you need to (e.g. know the public transport route or get the number of a taxi company).

Airbnb

If you haven't heard of Airbnb [http://airbnb.com], you've probably been living under a rock for the last couple of years! It's somewhat of a cross between Couchsurfing (well, a more upmarket version of Couchsurfing – you're paying, after all) and renting a flat, and hotel owners everywhere are up in arms because it's undercutting their profits with its popularity, which is why it's been splashed all over the news.

Anyone can sign up and put their flat (all or part of it) for rent. They might just rent out a spare room, in which case it's a bit like Couchsurfing or a B&B, or they might put up a whole spare apartment for rent. You can select when searching whether you'd rather see rooms to rent, or entire apartments, depending on whether or not you want to stay on your own/ have the whole apartment to yourself, and how much you want to pay. If staying in a room, again you may want to search for vegetarians or vegans (in the extra/keyword search field), or email the host and mention that you're vegan, to see if they can accommodate you. You can also see whether you'll have access to the kitchen and/or fridge – useful as a backup plan and place to cook and store your soy milk/snacks.

Be sure to read up on safety concerns (see the warning in the Couchsurfing section above) and take precautions to protect yourself. Also be aware that in some cities like Barcelona, Airbnb has come under fire from local renters, who complain that apartments are being turned into overpriced holiday rentals, thereby driving up prices for rentals being rented out to the local market. Some municipalities have even made Airbnb illegal, so be sure to research the legalities and local feelings toward Airbnb at your destination.

Housesitting

One popular way of traveling, particularly amongst long-term travelers, is housesitting. If you haven't heard of housesitting, it's exactly as it sounds. You look after someone's house (and sometimes pets) while they're on vacation or sabbatical, often for free. It's an excellent way to travel for free, although I've heard it can be hard to get started. (Who wants to leave their house in the hands of someone completely new, without any reviews?) If you know anyone who does housesitting, you could ask them to help you get started, and possibly refer you to someone. Be sure to ask them for a good review! The most popular site is Trusted Housesitters [http://www.trustedhousesitters.com/].

Vegvisits

A promising new site is Vegvisits, which has not launched at the time of writing. It is similar to Airbnb, for vegetarians, vegans, and others with special dietary requirements. You can stay with local vegetarians and vegans, and will be able to search by diet (e.g. vegetarian, vegan, raw, gluten-free). Also, interestingly, you'll be able to search by what appliances they have in their kitchen (blender, juicer, food processor) – which could be incredibly useful if you like to start off your day with a green juice or a smoothie bowl!

Renting an Apartment

This is one of my favorite options. If you're staying somewhere for a week or more, you can usually rent an apartment at a decent price – less than a hotel – and sometimes it even works out at a similar price to a private room in a hostel. The longer you stay, the cheaper it is. Have a look on TripAdvisor, Airbnb (remember to filter for whole apartments), and Homeaway. You might also want to look for local sites.

You might assume that all apartments have ovens or even ranges, and then go there to discover there's a hot plate-type setup (common in some smaller apartments rented in some locations). If you're planning to use the kitchen much, you'll want to make sure it has an oven or at least a range, plus a fridge, a microwave, and maybe a freezer if you'll need it. Also, most places come with basic cooking equipment, cutlery and plates, but it's worth making sure! Check by emailing the owner and verifying what cooking facilities and equipment are available.

More than likely, you'll find your apartment options limited in between looking at budget, number of rooms, Wi-Fi, kitchen facilities and location, but if you do somehow find yourself spoilt for choice, bust out that vegan restaurant map again on HappyCow/Google and see if you can nab an apartment near some vegan restaurants or stores!

* * *

Section 5:

Preparing for Your Trip.

• •

So, you've decided where to stay, made a list of restaurants and phrases and decided where to stay. Don't leave just yet! Once you've chosen a place to stay, your next step is picking what to pack! I'm not talking first aid kits here (pack one of those anyway, though). We're going to cover eco-friendly and vegan-friendly toiletries that are also travel-friendly. We'll be focusing on emergency food supplies to make your vegan travel easier. Plus we'll talk about eating on airplanes.

What to Pack: Toiletries

Ah, the toiletry bag, bane of every plane traveler's existence! Things have gotten a little bit complicated for those of us who fly with carry-ons, now that there are so many rules about what we can take on the plane – and how much of it. That's especially true for those of us who want to take eco-friendly and vegan toiletries, and can't just run to the nearest drugstore and buy a big pile of mini Colgate toothpastes and tiny bottles of Pantene. The easiest option is to simply buy some empty bottles that are travel-sized/TSA-approved, and fill them with your favorite shampoos, soaps etc. You can easily refill these before each trip, so you're not wasting lots of tiny plastic bottles.

Toothpaste, on the other hand, is more of an issue. You can't pick up refillable toothpaste tubes at your nearest drugstore, but you can order these refillable, BPA-free tubes on Amazon (also great for packing sunscreen!):

US orders: http://amzn.to/1SVzqBR

Or, you can buy little tubes of Jason brand natural toothpaste:

US orders: http://amzn.to/1R0gyTK
UK orders: http://bit.ly/1NndTnx

I'd also highly recommend checking out the hair and body care products at Lush, if you have a store nearby or can order online. They clearly label which products are vegan, and all their products are natural and many are made fresh. They have some non-liquid products like face soap/scrub in plastic tubs, solid perfumes, solid shampoo bars, bath bombs (solid balls which dissolve in water into bubbles), solid massage bars (which melt when heated to skin temperature) and more. These are great because you can stock up without worrying about going over your liquid limit! If you want to bring a treat along and are staying somewhere nice with a bathtub, Lush make excellent bath bombs and bath melts.

You might also want to check the contents of toiletries to ensure they are eco-friendly and free from parabens, SLS and other ingredients which have been implicated in causing health problems as well as environmental problems (some studies indicate that SLS may have a toxic effect on aquatic life). Many organic and vegan ranges are paraben and SLS free, but it's best to double-check anyway as this is not always the case.

If you're planning to travel for a while, you might need to do laundry, so don't forget to pack some laundry detergent. I find the best way to do this is to buy those laundry tabs (the solid ones), which transport well and, again, won't take you over your liquid limit. Or, you could buy a multi-purpose liquid like Dr. Bronner's soap, which you can use for just about everything – laundry, shower gel/soap, face soap, even toothpaste. Warning: I've never used it as toothpaste and the idea freaks me out a little, but by all means, try it and see what you think!

If you're traveling longer term, you might find yourself running out of toiletries. Check if there's a Lush nearby. Lush has expanded to a lot of locations and countries now! Or look for a local health food store. You may be able to buy a brand of your favorite stuff from back home. Be prepared to pay a lot more, and be prepared for it to taste really different. When I was in Taiwan, I bought some vegan, organic toothpaste from a brand that I regularly buy back home. However, instead of tasting minty fresh, this stuff tasted of salt! It made for a really salty, strange toothbrushing experience!

On a side note, when choosing clothes for your trip: Those "travel clothes" you often see travel magazines and blogs talking about (you know, the ones that wick moisture, never smell, don't wrinkle and pretty much sound like magical clothes that wash themselves) are not always vegan. They quite often contain silk, so check the fabrics of anything before purchase.

What to Pack: Food

So if you're anything like me, you almost always have a few snacks buried in the bottom of your bag. You put them in there at some point thinking, "I better pack some extras in case I can't find vegan food before my meeting/near the museum/at Sam's party even though she specifically told me she'd be making vegan food for me." I don't know where this irrational fear came from because I've never actually been anywhere I can't find at least one vegan option (although it may be just a banana or a bag of nuts). I don't really think it has anything to do with a fear of being without vegan food, more of a fear of ending up in the countryside/in the middle of a zombie apocalypse without any food, period. It probably explains why my cupboards are stocked to the brim with a huge supply of beans, nuts and grains. Just in case of those zombies, you know. I'd definitely be the one of my friends whose house everyone would go to in order to survive. Anyway, I usually forget that I've stockpiled things in my bag, and at some point when cleaning out my handbag, discover an array of Nakd bars and bags of dried fruit and nuts. Oops.

It does pay, though, to bring a few emergency supplies with you on your trip, particularly in case of an unfortunate airplane incident. You know, one of those awful cases where they forget to bring your vegetarian or vegan meal even though you ordered it in advance, and you dig in the bottom of your bag and discover that somehow this is the one time you DON'T have any bars. So you end up eating some Pringles you picked up in the airport as a treat, along with a slightly melted dark chocolate bar you found at the bottom of your bag (not the best dinner) while the flight attendants cackle (honestly, cackle) in the corner like the evil stepmother in a Disney princess movie and make fun of your sorry, sorry excuse for a dinner. Or wait, am I the only one that happened to? Well, suffice to say, I learned my lesson, and I now bring some food on all flights.

Yes folks, this happened – on an American Airlines flight. (I'm not afraid to name and shame.) Generally, American are pretty good with vegan meals, but this time they failed. Big time. When they came over and explained they'd forgotten my special meal, they offered me the vegetarian option of lasagne – a cheese-filled lasagne. No way that was going to be veganized! I explained that I didn't eat dairy, and the flight attendants seemed confused, then told me they didn't have any food to give me. So, I ended up eating Pringles and chocolate while the flight attendants laughed at me and commented snarkily, "That's an interesting dinner." (Yes, I did complain, and American did apologize, but that didn't really make up for it.) Moral of the story: Have a couple of backup bars, or something more substantial than Pringles.

This is particularly handy on cheap flights which don't provide meals. It also helps to avoid paying for excessively overpriced and often unhealthy meals in the airport. What's the key to packing a meal for the plane? Make something easily transportable, and also something that can be eaten cold, like a sandwich (but beware of sandwiches containing "pastes" like hummus – see note on liquids below). Bring along:

- Fruit (something that won't get crushed, like an apple, as opposed to berries which will just get smushed in your bag).

- Something relatively small and light which packs a lot of energy, like some nuts and seeds.

Remember not to bring any liquids or make sure that they are in smaller containers that won't take you over your liquid limit. And yes, airport officials often count "pastes" like hummus as liquid, as well as salad dressings.

Or you can make your own fruit and nut bars. Check out this super useful post from Oh She Glows with some great ideas and recipes for easily transportable snacks for the plane: http://bit.ly/1YplVxQ

Some airports also have a listing of different restaurants and stores by terminal, and you can use these to check if there are any places that you know have vegan options. For example, in UK airports there is often a Pret which offers a vegan sandwich option. There are Chipotle in some US airports, which offers vegan burritos.

Depending where you're going, and whether you're staying in a place with a kitchen where you plan to cook, you may want to bring along a few foods as well. If you're planning to cook, have a look at supermarkets and health food stores nearby, and find out if there are any foods you'll want which will be difficult to obtain. A few things worth considering taking:

- UHT/shelf stable soy milk (either one carton as a "starter" soy milk, so you at least have some for the first day, or in single packs if you're not going to have a fridge. You can use these single servings for breakfast each morning!).

- Powdered non-dairy coffee creamer or powdered soy milk (if you're going somewhere without a fridge, or you know you won't be able to buy soy milk in the location you're going. At least you can still have creamer in your coffee!).

  US orders: http://amzn.to/1SVEHt0

  UK orders: http://amzn.to/1lExhjy

- Instant ramen. (Try and find the healthiest brand possible, for example Koyo which is organic, vegan, made without MSG, and sold in many health food stores in the US and on Amazon: http://amzn.to/1X8UGdK.) You can make this easily if you have a kettle in your hotel room, or your hotel provides hot water for tea.

- Instant oatmeal cups or noodle cups. (Check ingredients to make sure they're vegan.) You can easily ask for hot water on the plane and have these as a snack!

- Fruit and nut bars, like Nakd/Clif/Lara/etc.

- Dark chocolate or other treats (if you have a sweet tooth and are going somewhere you won't be able to easily get vegan desserts).

- Nutritional yeast – if you like cooking with it and are going somewhere you can't easily buy it.

- Spice mix – this might make your cooking easier. The last thing you'll want to do is buy a bunch of spices for a kitchen you're only going to be using for a short period of time. I'd suggest picking one style of cooking and bringing a spice mix that is versatile, for example I like taking an Italian spice blend with me and using it to make pasta, sauté veg and make risotto/toppings for polenta, etc. Or, you can buy spice mixes for specific dishes like these ones for sale in the US, which are organic and come with a shopping list of fresh ingredients to pick up (e.g. chickpeas, tomatoes, and ginger): http://amzn.to/1X8UOtQ.

- Or you can even make your own spice mixes in plastic bags and bring them with you (tip: make sure your plastic bags are really well sealed so you don't end up with spices all over your bags! And be prepared for potential questions at security if you pack oregano).

- If you want to go all out you can come extra prepared like this traveling kitchen kit as described by Joy the Baker: http://bit.ly/1T9Y81U

You may also want to bring a portable set of cutlery, like the kind you can get for picnics or camping. (Just remember to pack it in your checked luggage!) Other useful kitchen tools to have on hand are a Swiss army knife or kitchen knife for chopping vegetables, scissors, a can opener, a vegetable peeler, and a corkscrew.

Eating on the Plane

Pretty much all major airlines offer vegan meals these days. On flights that serve meals, that is. Shorter flights and continental flights normally don't – check your booking. You'll need to book your meal when you book the tickets, or just after. You need to book it at least 48 hours in advance, but I'd recommend booking it as far in advance as possible, and double-checking at the desk when you check in to make sure they have it on your booking.

VGML is the international code for vegan meals. Occasionally, the Vegetarian Jain meal (VJML) or the Vegetarian Oriental meal (VOML) may also be vegan; you can check with your individual airline when booking.

Important: Keep in mind that often the condiments like salad dressing and margarine served with the meal may not be vegan! This is because usually the catering company will make the meal, and the flight attendants or other staff will later add the condiments – meaning they will add whatever is on hand, which is not necessarily vegan. Some airlines are more conscientious about condiments than others, but I'd recommend avoiding the condiments unless they are clearly marked vegan or you can check the ingredients.

As we've already discussed, I also always recommend bringing snacks and food (especially easily portable food and snack bars) with you on flights, in case they forget your meal. It can happen, and you don't want to be stuck on a plane for 10 hours with only some potato chips to eat!

* * *

Section 6:

What to Do When You Get There.

● ●

We've covered researching and finding restaurants, where to stay, and what to pack. This last section is all about what to do when you get there – from making friends, to how to order at non-vegan restaurants, to what to do if you're traveling with non-vegans.

It will also cover picking vegan activities and what to do if you get stuck and can't find anywhere to eat.

Making Friends

Depending on how long you're staying in a place, how long you're traveling for (if you're going multiple places) and whether you're traveling with friends/a partner/family, you may be more or less inclined to make friends in your destination. If you're traveling for a while, or you're on your own, you'll probably want to meet people – but no matter what your circumstances, arranging to meet like-minded people who live in your destination is a great way to make new friends and learn about local culture.

You can use some of the methods listed earlier, such as Couchsurfing and Meetup, to contact people with shared interests. Hostels are another classic way to meet people. Check reviews to see what sort of atmosphere the hostel has. Some hostels may be "party" destinations or have chilled hangout areas where you can meet people, while others tend to be used strictly for sleeping, with guests who are not very inclined to mix with others. As long as a hostel has a common area or a kitchen, though, you are likely to meet people.

You can also meet people on trains, or on walking tours (in many cities, you can find free ones, just Google or ask your hostel's front desk!). I've even met people in restaurants, when someone at a table nearby struck up a conversation – also a great way to meet local vegetarians and vegans! Keep an open mind and your best asset is a friendly smile. As long as you seem open, you don't necessarily even need to be outgoing – people will often just start conversations with you if you are traveling alone. If you're in a group, you'll likely need to make more of an effort to start conversations.

If You're Traveling with Non-Vegans

"Okay," you're thinking. "It's all well and good finding a list of amazing vegetarian and vegan restaurants I want to go to, and salivating over their menus. But my friends/grandma/boyfriend won't want to go there with me! They'll refuse and I'll be left to dine on lettuce in some meaty restaurant they choose!" You have three methods here:

1. Convince your meat-eater(s) to go to vegetarian or vegan restaurants
2. Go to non-vegetarian restaurants with them (and try to find vegetarian or vegan options)
3. Go for meals separately.

For option A, you can start by taking them to restaurants and not telling them everything is vegetarian. This can work well, if you choose good restaurants, and convince them that maybe veggie/vegan food isn't so bad after all – in fact, it's downright delicious. You can even start before your trip by taking them to vegetarian restaurants around your city and showing them how good they are (pick the best restaurants, of course). This might not work well if you think they'll feel "tricked" by you taking them to a restaurant and not mentioning it's vegetarian. Judge according to their personality!

If they're adventurous types, you can pitch going to veggie restaurants as a way to try out new things. They might just discover some new favorite foods. If you stay in a place with a hotel, cook them a kick-ass vegetarian meal that they'll love one night. A lot of people might be scared of eating out at exclusively vegetarian restaurants but come round to it when they realise they're not missing out and veggie and vegan food is still delicious.

If they're really adamantly opposed to trying out vegetarian restaurants, you might find yourself a bit torn. In this case, you'll likely end up eating in non-vegetarian restaurants with them. Try and choose the most vegetarian-friendly ones in this case, if possible (e.g. ones with vegetarian and vegan options clearly labeled on the menu). I find in North America VegGuide is the best resource for finding these veggie-friendly restaurants. If you can't find these sorts of restaurants listed on HappyCow or VegGuide, try choosing a cuisine that normally has vegan-friendly options.

If you're really determined to try a particular vegetarian restaurant you've heard lots of positive things about, it can be frustrating if your travel companions don't want to try it. In this case, you might want to make a deal with them. Perhaps there's an activity they really want to do that you're not as fascinated by? I'm not saying do anything that would compromise your values, but if your partner desperately wants to visit the museum of ancient anchors made between 500 and 300 B.C., maybe you could make a deal that you go to that museum if they then accompany you to the restaurant of your choice in the evening.

Also remember that just because you're traveling together doesn't mean you have to do everything together. You can go off on your own, or meet new vegetarian and vegan friends (from Couchsurfing/Meetup) and try out those vegan restaurants you're dying to eat at. Sometimes it's good to get a break from your traveling companions, especially if you are traveling together for a long time and starting to get on each other's nerves!

How to Order At a Non-Vegetarian Restaurant

So, what if you have to go to a non-vegetarian restaurant, either because your traveling companions don't want to go to a vegetarian restaurant, or because you simply can't find any? Well first, choose the restaurant carefully, and try and choose a place where you are more likely to be able to find vegetarian and vegan options. Think: Italian, Indian, Chinese, Thai, Japanese, Ethiopian, Moroccan, Lebanese…

Second, be careful how you order. Be prepared to ask a set of questions, not just "is this vegan?" in case they don't know what vegan means. In Section 3, "Translations," we covered a list of common phrases and words to translate, so have these handy! You'll want to ask questions specific to the local cuisine. So for example, in India, ask whether a curry contains ghee – but no need to ask if it contains fish sauce (unless you're in a Thai restaurant in India).

Be aware that in some cultures, it's considered rude to say no, so they may lie and say yes, it is vegan – even if it's not. In some Asian cultures such as Thai culture, there's a strong culture of "saving face" which means it's considered bad form to say no. Read up on the local culture!

Don't assume that something is vegetarian or vegan just because it looks like it might be. Sometimes vegetable side salads will come garnished with cheese or bacon, even though that's not listed on the menu. Sometimes ramen may sound like it's all vegetable, but come topped with an egg, or be made with a stock that's not vegan. Make sure you ask questions.

However, don't be discouraged if the waiter says they don't have any vegetarian or vegan options – just ask whether they can make something for you! As long as you ask politely – and not in a demanding, expectant way – most restaurants are willing to adapt their dishes to make them fully plant-based (or even invent a new dish). Be appreciative of their efforts, and be sure to thank the restaurant staff for making a vegan dish! If the dish is really fantastic, write up a review on it afterwards, and consider submitting it to HappyCow!

For a little breakdown by type of cuisine and common vegan dishes (as well as common hidden non-vegan ingredients), see below:

- Mexican – Order a vegetarian burrito or fajita, make sure the beans aren't cooked with lard and the rice isn't cooked with meat stock, and make sure they hold the cheese and sour cream. Guacamole is usually vegan and delicious! Although always double-check ingredients – often guacamole sold in shops in the UK and France contains sour cream.

- Italian – Check that the pizza base doesn't contain any dairy, and that pasta doesn't contain egg. Ask them to hold the cheese and check they didn't use any meat making the sauce. A lot of traditional fruit gelatos are made without dairy or eggs (just check).

- Spanish – When eating tapas, order vegetarian like pan con tomate (tomato and olive oil coated bread), pimientos de padron (roasted peppers with olive oil and sea salt), escalavida (roasted eggplant, bell pepper and onion) and make sure it doesn't contain any cheese or ham. They're usually cooked in olive oil rather than butter (just check) so don't usually contain dairy unless by way of cheese. Some Spanish restaurants like to top everything with jamon (ham) so ask about that.

- Sandwich/wrap shops – Try getting a vegetarian sandwich topped with hummus or just vegetables, but make sure they hold the cheese, mayo or butter and check the bread doesn't contain dairy.

- Lebanese – Try falafel, hummus, and fattoush salad. Check it doesn't come topped with labne (yogurt), that any tahini sauce is just tahini (no dairy) and any flatbreads don't contain dairy.

- Greek – Try fava (yellow split pea spread) and a Greek salad, hold the feta cheese. Check it's made with olive oil (it usually is) and doesn't contain any cheese.

- Japanese – Weirdly, when in Japan, don't even bother trying to go into a standard restaurant and ordering vegetarian or vegan. They don't like modifying food, and put bonito fish flakes in loads of unexpected places. But outside Japan, Japanese restaurants can often be a great place to find vegetarian and vegan food. Try ordering vegetable sushi (just make sure they don't add mayonnaise), tempura (make sure there's no egg in the batter) or miso or ramen soup (check they don't use fish stock or add bonito flakes). If you're going to Japan, don't worry though – you can usually find vegetarian restaurants near Buddhist temples.

- Chinese – Similar to Japan, you won't have much luck getting a vegan meal in a non-vegetarian restaurant in China (again, try near Buddhist temples), but outside China you will likely be able to find vegetarian and vegan options. The good thing about Japanese, Chinese and other East Asian cuisines is that milk isn't a traditional ingredient, so if you can ensure you're getting a vegetarian option without meat or fish then it will probably be vegan too. Try ordering a vegetable, tofu or seitan dish – check they haven't added oyster sauce.

- Taiwanese – In Taiwan, your best bet is a vegetarian restaurant. Be aware that some of the mock meats may contain egg whites or milk protein, so it's best to stick to tofu, vegetables and other familiar and safe ingredients!

- Thai and Laotian – When in Thailand, try saying "jay" (it's a religious term for vegan, which some believe to be derived from the Jain religion, which seeks to avoid harm to animals at all costs, including sweeping the ground in front of your feet to avoid stepping on small insects). In Thailand, if you ask for "jay" food, they will often be able to make you vegan food. Laos, which shares a similar language to Thailand, also utilizes the word "jay". At Thai restaurants outside Thailand, have vegetable and tofu curries (make sure they haven't added shrimp paste or fish paste) and pad thai (hold the egg).

- Vietnamese and Cambodian – In Vietnamese restaurants outside Vietnam, try vegetable or tofu spring rolls (summer rolls). Check the dipping sauce doesn't contain fish sauce. Or try a vegetable pho (pho chay); check the stock is a vegetable stock. In Vietnam and Cambodia, you will likely have the best luck asking for Buddhist vegetarian food, by asking for "chay" food (notice the similarity to the Thai and Laotian word "jay?" Some believe the words to be related and to be derived from the Jain religion).

- Myanma (Burmese) – In Myanmar, the word "thatalo," which translates to "lifeless" in the Burmese language, will get you vegetarian food in many restaurants.

- Korean – Try jap chae, a dish of vegetables and glass noodles (make sure they don't add any meat) or bibimbap (make sure they don't add egg or beef).

- Indian – Indian food is usually very good for vegetarians because of the large vegetarian population in India; however, to make it vegan, you'll need to ask they leave out dairy from cooking. Eggs aren't usually a problem as they aren't traditionally considered vegetarian. Try a vegetable curry dish with rice. Make sure they don't use ghee – clarified butter, which is commonly used to cook curries; just ask them to use vegetable oil instead! Naan usually is cooked in butter or contains yogurt so if you want bread ask them which of their breads are free from dairy.

- Turkish – Try mezze (small plates, like tapas, which are frequently vegetarian or vegan). Dishes that are usually vegan include patlican salatasi, a smoky grilled eggplant salad, muhammara, a spicy walnut and pepper dip, or imam biyaldi, eggplant stuffed with tomatoes, onion and garlic.

- Moroccan – From what I've read, eating vegetarian in Morocco isn't always easy, but at Moroccan restaurants in the US you can often count on a vegetable tagine and couscous. (Check it's all vegetable and doesn't contain chicken stock, beef stock, or butter.)

- Ethiopian (and Eritrean) – Ethiopia has a tradition of vegetarianism (veganism or near-veganism, apart from the occasional appearance of butter) during Lent and in the cases of strict Ethiopian Orthodox followers, Wednesdays and Fridays. Therefore, in a lot of Ethiopian restaurants, you'll find a wide selection of vegan or near-vegan dishes. They might not call it vegan or vegetarian, but if you ask for the fasting food, you can usually get some vegetarian and vegan food! Just make sure the dishes don't contain cheese, yogurt or butter. Try a bayenetu, a selection of vegetable curry dishes (anything "wat" is delicious) on top of injera, a traditional Ethiopian spongy bread made with teff flour, which some are saying will become the new quinoa. Injera bread is cultured like a sourdough and has a lemony flavor. It's traditionally used as both a plate and utensil, using it to scoop up the delicious curries. Eritrean restaurants typically have similar vegan options.

- Egyptian – koshari (a blend of pasta, macaroni, lentils, chickpeas and rice) and ful medammas (cooked and mashed fava beans) are usually vegan (check they use oil, and not butter or ghee, in cooking). In terms of desserts, halva is usually vegan.

- Eastern European – there's a tradition of veganism or near-veganism during Lent and before Christmas in many Eastern European Orthodox countries, such as Bulgaria, Romania and Russia. If you visit during this time of year, you will find many vegan Lenten delights! If you visit outside the Lent season, you may have better luck explaining your veganism by relating it to Lent. Beware that Lenten food may contain honey. You'll want to find out the local word for "fasting food" (in Romanian, for example, "mancare de post", or "nistisimo" in Greece).

Vegan Activities

When traveling, you'll probably want to make sure your activities align with your values. This means evaluating situations carefully. For example, you'll want to avoid some activities which are incredibly cruel: Thailand's famous tiger visits and elephant rides, visits to Seaworld, circuses or zoos in other cities. If you want to see animals in the wild, for example on safari, evaluate the program carefully to make sure it's cruelty-free, and the animals really are wild and allowed to roam free. You may want to even go a step further, and combine your travels with supporting and helping animals abroad. For example, you could volunteer in an animal sanctuary, donate to a local animal charity, or volunteer to help out at this elephant sanctuary in Thailand: http://www.elephantnaturefoundation.org/go/park.

You could also donate to an eco charity or offset your air miles. (Check that the offset program is doing what they say!) Or better yet, see if you can do the journey by train.

What To Do If You Get Stuck

Sometimes, no matter how many restaurants you look up before, no matter how many maps you memorize or menus you know by heart, circumstances conspire against you.

It was boiling hot, mid August, and our first ever visit to Sicily.

My boyfriend at the time and I had just arrived that day, and after having stocked our holiday apartment with goodies from the nearby supermarket, we raced towards our destination: a vegan bar/cafe/restaurant I'd heard nothing but incredible things about. But when we arrived, we were sorely disappointed to see a sign outside saying it was closed for "ferragosto", or August vacations. Undaunted, we went to another vegetarian restaurant nearby that I'd found on HappyCow. It, too, was closed for ferragosto. One by one, we discovered the handful of restaurants on HappyCow were closed, as were the ones I'd also discovered on Palermo Vegetariana, a free Google map of vegetarian restaurants in the city that I'd found.

Also listed on Palermo Vegetariana were some non-vegetarian restaurants, but none were Italian – and I really wanted to eat Italian food in Italy. I wasn't completely backed into a corner, because we had a kitchen in our rented apartment, so I had the option of cooking meals with delicious produce made from local markets. However, I did really want to eat out sometimes. I was on holiday, after all! I thought if worst came to worst we'd go to a restaurant and I'd enquire about vegan or veganizable options. We'd encountered so few people who spoke English, though, that I wasn't sure I'd be able to get my point across.

Desperate, the next day I emailed the contact email listed on Palermo Vegetariana. I didn't receive a reply. I did, however, receive a Facebook friend request from someone in Palermo. To this day I'm not sure if it was the founder of Palermo Vegetariana (as I suspect) or a coincidence, but I accepted the request. Shortly thereafter, I was friended by a restaurant called Tartaruga (Turtle). I Googled the name and found page after page of articles describing the new restaurant, which had only opened a few days before, as a slow food restaurant. Knowing that slow food restaurants are often vegetarian or have vegetarian options, I looked for some more information on Tarturaga. After digging a bit deeper, I discovered that Tarturaga was, in fact, fully vegetarian with vegan options.

I sent a Facebook message to my new restaurant friend on Facebook, asking if they were open that evening and if I could book a table for two and received a reply: "No English. Yes 19:00 table for tree [sic]." Slightly dubious but nonetheless curious, we set off for the restaurant at 19:00 and were greeted by Laura, the friendliest woman in the world, who welcomed us into her restaurant, and to Sicily, with open arms. Although she didn't speak much English, we were able to communicate enough by way of pointing at various dishes and asking "vegano?" That first night, she brought us free dessert and a sample of some vegan cheese she'd been working on (and hadn't yet put on the menu). We went back four more times during our visit. Also, the founder of Palermo Vegetariana finally replied to me and told me about one other vegetarian restaurant that was open, but told me pretty much everything else on the island was shut for August vacation. We visited the other restaurant but we were drawn back to Tartaruga, and especially Laura, over and over. She plied us with free food and drink, but it wasn't just that, or the fact that we wanted to support a new local vegetarian business — it was just that we felt so damn welcome!

Morning
Sicily, Italy
2013

This is one of the best things about travelling as a vegan, I find – once you meet another one you feel connected as part of the vegan community, and more often than not they welcome you with open arms and take care of you. I'll never forget Laura's hospitality.

So what's the best thing you can do if you're stuck? Reach out – to anyone in your network – and try to find someone local who's vegetarian or vegan, or some connection. Even if you don't know a local vegetarian website, look for vegetarians or vegans on social networks (Facebook, Twitter, vegetarian networks like Volentia), Couchsurfing, etc. Ask your connections if they know of anyone (you might find a friend of a friend of a friend). Try to find a local health food store, or if there aren't any, try to find an area of town where alternative types hang out, like near a university, and you might have more luck. This is also why it's helpful to stay somewhere with a kitchen. But if you don't have one, then go into local restaurants and explain that you're vegan (or show them a translation in the local language) and what you can and can't eat. Most people in most places in the world will help out if they can!

And if you're really stuck and can't find anywhere, read on for some recipes, some of which can be made with just a coffeemaker, or without any equipment.

* * *

Section 7:

Emergency Recipes for the Road: Food to Cook Anywhere.

• •

If you are staying somewhere with a kitchen, this last section is for you. Here are a handful of simple recipes you can make in a small or limited kitchen (or in the case of a couple recipes, in an electrical drip brew coffeemaker, the kind common in the US).

Useful Tools to Have With You

- Reusable or disposable bowls and/or plates. Plates can double as chopping boards! Try using the ironing board as a work surface if you don't have a table or desk, or need more space.

- Pocket knife/Swiss army knife for chopping

- Reusable or disposable cutlery Try these:
  US orders: http://amzn.to/1OsgwS0
  UK orders: http://amzn.to/1lKoCvU

- Scissors

- Can opener

- Vegetable peeler

- Corkscrew

- Useful items if your hotel room contains one:

- Coffeemaker or kettle

- Microwave

————— Recipes ———⟶

Soup in a Coffeemaker

Equipment needed: coffeemaker, bowl and spoon

1. Supermarket: Buy a can of your favorite soup.

2. In hotel: Turn on the coffeemaker. Pour the soup into the glass coffee pot and turn on, but don't fill any water in the water filter (unless you want to water down your soup). The hot plate under the glass coffee pot will heat up your soup.

Salad

Equipment needed: plate, fork and knife

1. Supermarket: Pick up some lettuce and your favorite vegetables, plus a can of beans of your choice. Look for miniature bottles of vinegar and olive oil for the dressing.

2. In hotel: Wash veg in bathroom sink, chop vegetables on the plate with your knife. Arrange on the plate, top with dressing and you're done!

*Please be careful and only do this in countries where the water is safe! In countries where the drinking water is not safe (e.g. India) do NOT buy and consume raw, uncooked vegetables.

Couscous in a coffeemaker

Equipment needed: hotel room coffeemaker or kettle, bowl, plate and fork or spoon.

1. Supermarket: Buy couscous, your favorite vegetables and beans, and a sauce or spice mix if you want.

2. In hotel room: Heat water in the coffeemaker until as close to boiling as possible, then pour over a bowl of couscous. Put the plate on top of the bowl so the couscous cooks for several minutes. You can steam vegetables as well, in an inch or so of water in the glass coffee jar. Put them on the heat until they have steamed through. Add beans and you have a filling meal!

Bean Burritos

Equipment needed: plate, knife, possibly a can opener

1. Supermarket: Buy tortillas, a can of refried beans (get one with an easy-open top if possible, or ask at hotel reception if they have a can opener you can borrow), black olives, tomatoes, salsa, avocado.

2. In hotel room: This one's so simple! Chop up your olives and tomatoes and slice your avocado. Put it all in the tortilla and roll it up!

Avocado on Toast

Equipment needed: toaster, plate, bowl, knife

1. Supermarket: Buy bread and avocado, and, if you're feeling fancy, a lemon.

2. In hotel room: If you don't have a toaster and are staying in a hotel, check if there's a toaster in the breakfast room they'll let you use. Or I've read (but be careful because this sounds kind of dangerous!) you can toast on an iron if your hotel has an iron and ironing board.

3. Toast the bread, cut the avocado and mash in the bowl. Put the mashed avocado on the toast and top with a sprinkle of lemon juice.

Oatmeal in a Coffeemaker

Equipment needed: hotel room coffeemaker, bowl, spoon

1. Supermarket: oats.

2. In hotel room: Put the oats and water in the coffeemaker, heat until cooked.

Sandwiches

PB & J, hummus and tomato slices, vegetable pate, tofu (like the pre-cooked and marinated Taifun variety you can get across Europe) & vegetables

Equipment needed: plate, knife

1. Supermarket: bread or wrap and your favorite fillings.

2. In hotel room: Make the sandwich. (Does this require any more explanation?)

Baked Potato in a Microwave

Equipment needed: microwave, knife, plate, fork

1. Supermarket: Potatoes, toppings (I suggest vegetarian baked beans without pork – British-style!)

2. In hotel room: Wash the potato, dry and prick several times with the prongs of a fork. Heat potato in the microwave for 5 minutes. Turn over and cook for another 4-5 minutes until soft. Remove, slice open and add toppings and return for another 1-2 minutes until the toppings are heated.

One-pot Pasta

Equipment needed: one pot, knife, plate or chopping board, plate to eat, fork

Best done in a hostel or holiday apartment kitchen.

1. Supermarket: olive oil, 8oz pasta in your favorite shape, 1½ cups of vegetable stock or water, cherry tomatoes, garlic, onion, basil, vegetables of your choice.

2. In your hotel or apartment kitchen: Chop up the garlic, tomatoes and vegetables.

3. Add the oil to your pot and heat over medium heat. Add the garlic and onion and sauté until just browned.

4. Add the tomatoes, stock/water and pasta and bring to a boil. Stir to submerge the pasta.

5. Reduce the heat to medium-low and cover, adding the other vegetables according to how long it will take them to cook through. You need to cook the pasta for around 7-9 minutes or until the pasta is al dente (look at the instructions on the package). Sprinkle basil on top and serve.

Chili

Equipment needed: microwave, bowl, can opener, plate, knife

1. Supermarket: can of kidney beans, pinto beans or other beans as desired, onion, garlic, can of chopped tomatoes, chilli powder and cumin powder

2. In hotel room: Chop onion and garlic and add to the bowl. Add the rest of the ingredients to the bowl and microwave for 5 minutes. Stir and microwave another 3-4 minutes.

Snack: Hummus with Dip-able Items

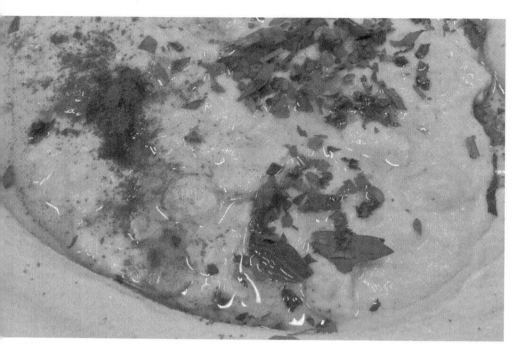

Equipment needed: None

Buy a tub of hummus, a loaf of crusty French bread, crackers, vegetable sticks, or cherry tomatoes. Dip and enjoy – simple!

Snack: Trail mix

Equipment needed: None or a plastic bag

Buy a mix of different nuts, seeds and dried fruits (plus some dark chocolate or cacao nibs if you want a treat) and mix up in a plastic bag. This is best done by buying small portions of each from a bulk bin.

Instant Food

Last idea!

Buy some of these from Trader Joe's and heat in the microwave or by submerging the packet in hot water from the coffeemaker or kettle: http://amzn.to/1XlozCd.

* * *

Section 8:

Final Tips & Resources.

If you are staying somewhere with a kitchen, this last section is for you. Here are a handful of simple recipes you can make in a small or limited kitchen (or in the case of a couple recipes, in an electrical drip brew coffeemaker, the kind common in the US).

After Your Trip

By now, you've hopefully had an excellent trip full of delicious vegan food. Once you're home, don't forget to share your experiences with others! Help out future vegan travelers by leaving reviews on TripAdvisor, HappyCow or Foursquare. If you discover a new vegan restaurant, you can submit it to HappyCow.

If you have a blog, writing up a post about your trip, including information about the restaurants you visited, what vegan dishes they had, and how the food was, might inspire and assist other vegans.

If you used information from any blogs, or got information from people on social media, thank them! You might think that they're too busy to care about your messages, but everyone likes to be thanked. They've put in the effort of putting together blog posts or information for you, so let them know it helped you.

If you discovered any restaurants that have closed, let the blogger know, and report it to HappyCow and TripAdvisor.

Last, tell others (vegan and non-vegans alike) about your experiences, and dispel the myth that vegan travel is difficult and boring and involves long slogs through the streets looking for food, or eating nothing but canned chickpeas!

Resources

HappyCow
happycow.net

VegGuide
vegguide.org

VegDining
vegdining.com

HappyCow App
iOS ($3.99): bit.ly/happycowitunes
Android ($2.99): bit.ly/happycowapp

VeganXpress App
iOS ($1.99): bit.ly/veganxpress

Vegman App
iOS (free): bit.ly/vegmanapp

North American Vegetarian Society (NAVS)
navs-online.org

Couchsurfing
couchsurfing.com

Meetup
meetup.com

Post Punk Kitchen Forums

forum.theppk.com

Vegan Forum

veganforum.com

iBarnivore

iOS (free): bit.ly/ibarnivore

Vegaholic

iOS ($1.99): bit.ly/vegaholic

VegeTipple

Android ($1.99): bit.ly/vegetipple

Evernote

evernote.com

Pocket

getpocket.com

Doodle

doodle.com

European Vegan Zine

bit.ly/euveganzine

Vegan Passport

bit.ly/veganpassport4

Hotels.com
hotels.com

Lastminute
lastminute.com

Hotel Tonight (App)
iOS (free): bit.ly/hoteltonightitunes
Android (free): bit.ly/hoteltonightandroid

Hostel World
hostelworld.com

Hostel Bookers
hostelbookers.com

Vegetarian Guides (to London, France, Europe, etc.)
vegetarianguides.co.uk

Airbnb (please note this is a referral, so if you sign up and use the service you will receive a $20 voucher and so will I)
airbnb.co.uk/c/caitling58?s=8

Vegvisits
vegvisits.com

TrustedHousesitters
www.trustedhousesitters.com

Tripadvisor
tripadvisor.com

Homeaway

homeaway.com

Lush

lush.com

Pocket

getpocket.com

Wikitravel

wikitravel.org

Is it Vegan? (App) – you can scan a barcode and it will tell you if the product is vegan (best results in the US)
iOS ($4.99): bit.ly/isitveganapp
Android: bit.ly/isitveganandroid

Vegetarian London (book)
bit.ly/veglondon

Vegetarian Paris (book)
bit.ly/vegparis

Vegetarian Britain (book)
bit.ly/vegbritain

Vegan Guide to NYC (book)
bit.ly/veganguidenyc

Top Vegan Restaurants Worldwide

(Source, HappyCow.net rankings, as of November 2015)

1. The Veggie Grill – Hollywood, California, USA
2. Nanuchka – Tel Aviv, Israel
3. Harvest at The Bindery – Portland, Oregon, USA
4. Three Carrots Restaurant – Indianapolis, Indiana, USA
5. Cuenco – Mendoza, Argentina
6. Krawummel – Munester, Germany
7. The Veggie Grill – San Jose, California, USA
8. Atsumi Raw Café – Phuket, Thailand
9. The Veggie Grill – El Segundo, California, USA
10. Loving Hut – Menton, France

With thanks to HappyCow.net for allowing us to use this data. Accurate as of November 2015.

Top Vegan Destinations of 2016

Berlin, Germany

Berlin is fast becoming known as a vegan capital of the world. With 26 fully vegan restaurants and counting, Berlin has something that will suit all tastes – from raw and healthy newcomer Café Laauma to vegan creperie Let it Be. Berlin is also home to "vegan street" (Schivelbeinerstrasse), a block-long stretch in Prenzlauerberg which hosts Avesu, a vegan shoe shop, Dear Goods, a vegan clothing and bag store, Veganz, a vegan supermarket and the attached Goodies Café.

London, England

England was the birthplace of Donald Watson, The Vegan Society and the vegan movement, and London is naturally host to a large vegan scene. From old favourites like Manna (London's oldest vegetarian restaurant, now turned vegan) to Mildred's (an extremely popular vegetarian restaurant in Soho, which always necessitates a long wait to get a table), and now newcomers like Kabaret @ Karamel, a vegan bar, London has a thriving vegan scene. London also boasts the largest vegan social group in the world, the London Vegan Meetup [www.meetup.com/londonvegan/], which has vegan events nearly every day.

San Francisco, California, USA

From the hippies of Haight-Ashbury in the 60s to the gay scene in recent years, San Francisco has always had a progressive vibe. Nowadays, San Francisco is notable for its vegan scene. Millennium Restaurant, considered by some to be the best vegan restaurant in the world, is located in Oakland, just outside San Francisco. San Francisco also boasts gems like Gracias Madre, a vegan Mexican restaurant, as well as being the headquarters of vegan magazine VegNews.

Taipei, Taiwan

Taipei might not be the first city that springs to mind when considering vegan destinations, but with some reports saying forty percent of the population practices vegetarianism at least part of the time (mainly for religious reasons, following Buddhist practices), it's very vegetarian- and vegan-friendly. Vegetarian restaurants grace nearly every block, so you're never far from veggie food. Buffet restaurants are popular, and for breakfast you can pick up fresh-cut tropical fruit from a market or a fruit stall on the street. Beware that mock meats may contain egg or milk extract, so best to steer clear of those and stick with well-known dishes (like vegetable or tofu) unless you can confirm. Food is also inexpensive compared to the U.S. or Western Europe, and you can dine in high-class style at Yu Shan Ge, popular with Taiwanese celebrities, and eat a 9-course meal for around $30.

New York City, New York, USA

In New York, you can find just about any cuisine you'd ever want — including a huge selection of vegetarian and vegan food. From a vegan cheese shop, Dr. Cow Tree Nut Cheese, to a vegan shoe shop, Moo Shoes, New York has it all. Want a vegan coat? Vaute Couture, a high-end vegan coat line, is also based in New York. And naturally, you can dine on some of the best vegan food in the world at restaurants like Candle 79.

Glasgow, Scotland

Glasgow was named the UK's most vegan-friendly city by PETA in 2013. Glasgow boasts everything from fully-vegan bars like the Flying Duck and Mono to vegan haggis fritters (non-vegan haggis is made from sheep's stomach) at Saramago Café.

Chiang Mai, Thailand

While "jay" restaurants ("jay" is the Thai Buddhist form of vegetarian/vegan which normally excludes garlic and onion as well as animal products) abound throughout Thailand, Chiang Mai, with its large expat population, is also home to raw food restaurants, macrobiotic cafes, and healthy salad bars. Thailand also holds a vegetarian festival every year over a ten-day period, normally falling in September or October. Some participants engage in self-mutilation as a form of religious rite (for example piercing their cheeks with knives), and vegan food is widely available throughout the festival period, with many restaurants and street vendors selling "jay" food, as many people go vegetarian for the duration of the holiday. Phuket is said to have the widest and best selection of vegan food at this time.

Barcelona, Spain

Barcelona's vegan scene is growing quickly and surprising many in a land that worships chorizo and jamon (ham, which is liberally put on just about everything in Spain). In addition to old favorites like upscale restaurant Teresa Carles, Barcelona's burgeoning vegan scene now counts a vegetarian and vegan pizzeria, Dolce Pizza y los Veganos, a vegan and mostly gluten-free bakery, Pastisseria La Besneta, a vegan shoe shop, Amapola, and four vegan grocery stores.

Portland, Oregon, USA

Birthplace of the vegan mini mall, which houses a vegan grocery, a vegan bakery, and a vegan tattoo parlor, Portland has long been hailed a vegan mecca. From vegan food carts to vegan donuts to a vegan strip club (yes, really), Portland really does have it all – vegan-style. It's also fairly standard to encounter vegan options on most non-vegetarian restaurant menus.

* * *

Thank you!

Thank you so much for reading this, and I hope it has come in handy! If you want to get in touch or share your travel tales, you can reach me on caitlin@theveganword.com.

If you enjoyed, please tell your vegetarian or vegan friends and family about it. I'd also like to ask you to share a review on Amazon – because of the Amazon algorithm, the more reviews that appear on Amazon, the more Amazon recommends this book to customers. And the more Amazon recommends the book, the more people can take stress-free, totally vegan vacations (and not resort to eating chickpeas from a can, or worse – give up being vegan on the road because they think it's not feasible!).

Acknowledgments

I'd like to thank everyone who helped me with this book, for giving up their evenings and weekends and free time to help me. I'd especially like to thank my friend and brilliant designer, Umit Koseoglu, who did the front cover, and Loki Lillistone, for the beautiful layout design. I also want to extend a huge thanks to my team of readers for their invaluable feedback and advice:

Alison Classe
Gillian Pollock (Guid Publications)
Cadry Nelson (cadryskitchen.com)
Rika (veganmiam.com)
Joey (flickingthevs.blogspot.com)
Nikki Scott (South East Asia Backpacker, South America Backpacker and Europe Backpacker)

And last, I'd like to thank my puppy, Benito, for reminding me when it was time to stop writing and take him for a walk outside in the sun

Made in the USA
San Bernardino, CA
12 February 2016